# UNDERSTANDING MENTAL ILLNESS
## 5TH EDITION

## MARIANNE RICHARDS

# Dedication

Margaret Vera Richards.
RIP

# Disclaimer

This book is neither for self diagnosis nor treatment. Those worried about mental health should seek Psychiatric help.

# UNDERSTANDING MENTAL ILLNESS
## CONTENTS

PP

Introduction

Ch1.  Drawing the Line: Sanity - Insanity                9

Ch 2.  Mental Health and Communities                    23

Ch 3.  A History of Mental Illness to the 17th century   33

Ch 4.  Mental Illness 18th- 20th Century                 47

Ch 5.  The Mental Health Act 1983                        67

Ch 6.  From Detection to Diagnosis                       75

Ch 7.  Talking Cures                                     81

Ch 8.  Modern Medical Treatments                         88

Ch 9.  Pen Portraits of Therapists                       109

Ch 10. Institutional Care and Support Groups             135

Ch 11. Case Histories                                    141

Ch 12. Social and Complementary Approaches               177

Ch 13. Reflections                                       189

Further Information
Glossary
Index

# Introduction

This book is a broad ranging introduction to mental illness for beginners. In jargon free language it answers typical questions about the nature of mental illness, its symptoms, and an overview of the experience of mental illness with its often bizarre symptoms.

This is a journey through detection, diagnosis and treatment explaining why mental illness is difficult to diagnose and offering a brief historic overview. Also covered are the process of new drug trials, how medication works and an overview of some complementary treatments.

To make the experience realistic and lighten the text I have written fictional 'day in the life of' mental health professionals and case histories based on my clinical and personal experience and symptom clusters from DSMIV. It is good to remember though, that everyone's experience of mental illness is different and people respond differently to treatment.

This book is not for self-diagnosis. Readers or family worried about symptoms are advised to seek psychiatric help. There are many reasons for changes in mood or behavior not attributable to mental illness.

If readers have specific interests they would like to see in future editions they are welcome to contact me via the Publisher. This field is constantly changing and it is impossible to iron out all errors or include every bit of information. My aim is to be broad reaching and set the scene for your further exploration of this fascinating field. I hope you enjoy reading this book.

Marianne Richards
May 2012

# Chapter 1

## Drawing the Line: Sanity - Insanity

**Content of this Chapter:**
Intolerance and Prejudice
Moral Panics
Exclusion and Mental Illness
Language or Labelling
Feared Mental Illnesses
Exercise
Parameters for Acceptable Behaviour
Definition of States Requiring Intervention

Mental illness is hard to understand even if you have experienced it. In making the attempt it is important to take into consideration the backcloth of pre-conceived ideas and fears present in human communities. It is also vital to understand the difficulties of diagnosing from the professionals point of view. This chapter addresses these issues.

### Intolerance and Prejudice

Throughout history individuals who have not conformed to the expectations of society or tribe risked exclusion. Those wearing unconventional clothing, using language or behaviour different to that commonly used in the group, or rejecting accepted politics were at risk from ridicule, stigmatization or death depending on the tolerance levels of their society. These were not the only risks of living in groups.

In the sixteenth century millions of innocent men and women were charged with witchcraft and risked torture, imprisonment and burning.

The Catholic Church wielded huge power and witch hunting provided a way of maintaining it. For centuries Inquisitions wielded terrifying power over illiterate communities steeped in a common fear of curses and evil. Anyone offending a neighbour risked being falsely accused and brought before an Inquisition. If relatives of such wretches chose to comfort them as they burned, they were in danger of implication. This was a time when women feared to grow old lest their senile looks lead to an accusation of witchcraft. Beautiful women were branded witches through spite, old ones because of eccentricity or misdiagnosis of skin tags as *witch marks*.

In modern times there is little fear of witchcraft, hell and damnation but non-conforming individuals still risk being excluded for much the same reasons - fear, envy, spite, anger and all the negative human emotions. This is not confined to individual behaviour.

Totalitarian states maintain power by crushing opposition through false accusations, torture and murder. In such places those who oppose the regime risk being declared insane, imprisoned, force fed powerful psychiatric drugs or executed. Separated from family and friends many commit suicide rather than endure isolation.

Group behaviour was first analyzed by Sigmund Freud, Carl Jung and their descendants who uncovered many of the often unconscious reasons why humans can be cruel and irrational. We now know that the purpose of rejecting what appears to be abnormal behaviour, appearance or opinion serves to confirm the identity and safety of the group. On the other hand it can warn a group of impending attack.

In the 21$^{st}$ century whilst the cruelties of exclusion still exist in a myriad of forms, those with emotional intelligence are aware of why they do what they do. In this age of terrorism people need to be alert to dangerous individuals but this holds a risk of being over sensitive to everyone who might be, for example, Muslim or wear a beard or robes. There is now more scope for tolerance yet group pressure often precludes individual effort. We refer to these irrational fears as *moral panics.*

## Moral Panics

Recently in the UK a retired schoolmaster was wrongly accused of murdering a young female. The man in question was sporting what might appear alarmingly bushy long, white hair. Accusers indulged in public tittle-tattle about his mannerisms, habits and social behaviour based on irrational fears. Such was the moral panic the man had to go into hiding. After the real murderer was caught, the man reappeared. His long hair was now cut in respectable style, he wore a suit and walked next to a grim-faced barrister. Same man, same background, same lifestyle but viewed differently by his accusers who disappeared into the woodwork.

Take another example. Dr Harold Shipman, a respected GP of long standing working for decades alongside doctors, nurses, pathologists. For years the elderly were entrusted to his care by unwitting relatives. Shipman the pillar of society made a public interview about treatment of the mentally ill in the community. Then one day it struck an observant undertaker that there had been an extraordinary number of funerals among Shipman's patients. Although only charged for a small number of murders, a subsequent public enquiry suggested the number ranged between 250 and 400 making Shipman the most prolific serial killer.

Kind hearted, if worldly unwise Princess Diana was labelled with borderline personality disorder. Here was a gentle soul with a plethora of uncontrolled emotions who unwisely tried to control the powerful forces of the establishment and media. Her devoted public demanded news, unwittingly triggering a paparazzi frenzy which ultimately lead to her death. Shocked, the public colluded with her estranged brother to castigate those who had served them the gossip they craved. After her death there was soul-searching and guilt then an embarrassed forgetting as the story of her ill-fated memorial and badly starred love life emerged.

I wish to demonstrate how easy it is for the public to make itself judge and jury and this extends to those unfortunate enough to develop mental illness. Even professionals can be mislead.

### CONTINUUM theory

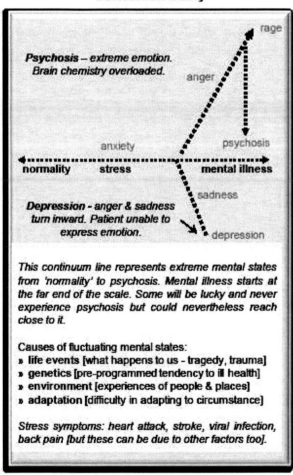

This continuum line represents extreme mental states from 'normality' to psychosis. Mental illness starts at the far end of the scale. Some will be lucky and never experience psychosis but could nevertheless reach close to it.

Causes of fluctuating mental states:
- life events [what happens to us - tragedy, trauma]
- genetics [pre-programmed tendency to ill health]
- environment [experiences of people & places]
- adaptation [difficulty in adapting to circumstance]

Stress symptoms: heart attack, stroke, viral infection, back pain [but these can be due to other factors too].

Most murders are committed by so-called sane people not those with a known mental disorder. However, this is not the thrust of this book.

## Exclusion and Mental Illness

Up to the early 20<sup>th</sup> century individuals were being incarcerated in Asylums sited well away from communities. These were not only people with active mental illness but so-called *social misfits* whose only problem might be eccentricity or what would now be considered minor social aberrations.

In the 1970's the UK Care in the Community Act forced the Asylums to close and patients were sent to live in group homes or social housing. Whilst there were instances of acceptance and tolerance other individuals became openly hostile.

One might ask who or what was to blame for the continuing stigma. A major flaw in the Care in the Community Act was a lack of public education in how to live with and understand those with enduring mental illness, which might have reduced fear.

There were good reasons for fear as there were a small number of people who represented a danger to the public if not constantly medicated and watched. Unfortunately the presence of media gives the public access to news which once might have been stemmed locally. Sensationalism sells newsprint and it is not always to the good for one-sided stories to be cast abroad about potentially dangerous people who in fact are not. But a human need for scapegoats around times of uncertainty fires imaginative articles, which prove devastating to individuals and their families.

Sometimes annoyance is understandable. If a neighbour is noisy or behaves in an unexpected way he or she is not easy to live with. Some individuals fail to take medication for a variety of reasons, a situation which rarely occurred in the confines of an Asylum but has become more common with community care.

## Language or Labelling

When a group of people are bent on excluding another, the first thing accentuated are the differences between the group and 'it'. One of the first ways is through the use of words or language which describes the individual in a negative way. Then comes false accusations for example, the Jews were accused of creating poor social conditions which existed in the German nation and this fear was exploited by Hitler and his thugs.

If an individual displayed odd behaviour such as shouting or talking to the self or more seriously committed an attack, local newspapers commonly referred to such persons as *mad, mental, crazy, schizo* or *psycho*. Mental health charities and Psychiatrists have been active for some years in discussions with influential media people in order to reduce the stigma around mental illness. Such negative words are thankfully more rare except in red top newspapers.

This bad publicity extends to sad cases where individuals commit suicide. As well as a common view of suicidal persons as being somehow selfish, they have been cruelly mocked on social websites. There is a growing understanding of depression as an illness rather than a choice. Newspapers have largely agreed not to publish details of the method to prevent so called copycat suicides.

Another modern phenomena is the tendency to refer to individuals by labels, for example schizophrenic rather than a person with schizophrenia. A diagnosis of schizophrenia was at one time tantamount to social suicide. Labelling is helpful only for diagnosis. Giving a name to a disorder allows a course of preventative action to be taken.

The latest view leans increasingly away from diagnostic labels and towards identifying and treating individual symptoms as they occur – thus, like having a cold, it is recognized that someone might experience a psychotic episode, receive treatment and return to life untainted by a permanent psychiatric label.

No one remains neurotypical their whole life, but fluctuate along a median line from mental health to mental ill health. It is therefore in everyone's interest to understand and prevent unjust labelling.

## Feared Mental Illnesses

It is true a tiny number of people with mental illness are dangerous because the nature of their illness makes it likely that they will commit criminal acts. Although it might not seem that way there are relatively few psychopaths.

A psychopath is born without moral capacity and cannot be blamed for actions in a moral sense. Nevertheless murderous psychopaths are locked away for the safety of the community. There is no cure for this disorder.

Similarly, a paedophile's lust for children is genetic. There is no cure except voluntary chemical castration. Such people need to be monitored and are placed on sex offender's registers when they are caught.

Drug addicts are likely to commit crime in order to fund their addiction because the physical need will overwhelm the side of their brain which is responsive to moral decisions.

A small number of people with schizophrenia might fail to take medication because they think there is nothing wrong with them or under a delusion of being poisoned. Under the influence of powerful delusions a few can become murderous. However, there are many people with this diagnosis who are successfully living relatively normal lives thanks to modern medications.

John Nash the great mathematician (his story is told in the film *A Beautiful Mind*) developed schizophrenia during his teens but lived a full life, had a happy marriage and was awarded the Nobel prize for his work on economic theory. He was able to overcome his symptoms using his powerful logical mind but his gift for this self-cure is unique.

In conclusion, contrary to popular belief there are few people with enduring mental illness who are dangerous. There are far more *bad* than *mad* people in this world to use that phraseology. Even among so called neurotypicals there are eruptions of greed, revenge, envy, spite and murderous rage. Lately there has been a spate of family men who have butchered wives and children before committing suicide. There have also been sprees of violence and arson carried out by youths under the excuse of under employment.

Usually knowledge breeds tolerance. Aside from those with personal experience or other motivated readers, how many people bother to read about mental illness? Few people realize how common mental illness is, that there are many types with varying severity, that episodes of illness flourish and disappear, still less that a large percentage of those diagnosed with major mental illnesses live normal lives without neighbours realizing.

## Exercise
Part 1

In a busy street you see a man dressed in ragged white robes muttering and pointing at the sky. A crowd gathers and someone calls the Police. Some people laugh, others turn away and continue shopping. A group of tourists take photographs. The Police arrive and arrest the man. Because he resists they handcuff him and bundle him into a car. This makes him angry and he starts shouting and foaming at the mouth.

Several witnesses attend a Court hearing where the man is charged with creating a public nuisance and resisting arrest. Consider what you have read and answer the following:

- *Would you consider this man's behaviour rational?*
- *Have you any sympathy?*
- *Would you try to help or turn away?*

Part 2

*Take each of the following statements in turn and ask the same questions if this man proved to be:*

- under the influence of drugs
- a classical musician who has had too much to drink
- a young man drunk on his coming of age
- seriously mentally incapacitated
- recently physically disabled through a car accident
- epileptic
- speaking in a religious fervour
- someone with a brief psychotic episode (nervous breakdown)

*Which conditions would make you feel more sympathetic and less likely to want the man locked up? Which do not change your opinion? Do you still believe him insane?*

Part 3

Our first witness says the man is dangerous and should be imprisoned. He maliciously claims the man hit someone. Another witness says this is not true and the man was reacting to someone lunging at him. The third witness is a Psychiatrist who diagnoses schizophrenia and recommends the man be detained in a secure Hospital for observation. The fourth witness is the leader of an Arts

Group who believes he has seen the man performing in a troupe of Street Actors in another town.

Our final witness is late. He rushes in with three other devotees. He translates for the Court that the man is their friend. They are a sect visiting a relative. In the cell below their friend has suffered an epileptic fit. The men are angry their friend has been maltreated. The man could not speak English and no translator has been made available.

It is easy to make judgments, to be intolerant, to read people through the lens of personal prejudices. Those with mental symptoms are more likely to be attacked or shunned because their symptoms are not understood and therefore likely to be feared.

## Parameters for Acceptable Behaviour
*Place*
The robed man's behaviour took place in public. His actions were not compatible with what would be normally acceptable in such a place. What is acceptable at an arts festival, opera house, formal dinner and a private home varies.

*Can we agree certain behaviours are either acceptable or unacceptable depending upon **where** they are committed and for what specific reason.*

*Time*
If the man continued to display his behaviour for hours or days would it increase the likelihood of his being diagnosed insane? If this behaviour continued for minutes then he walked away would the problem remain? *Perhaps insanity consists of a **time** frame.*

## Effect on Others
Our friend provoked a series of reactions. Whilst some people experienced him as benign he appears to have upset others. *Perhaps the **effect** on other people has to do with sanity too.*

## Ability to Survive

How long is it before a stray person is deemed incapable and taken into care? If this had been a child the time frame would have been shorter. *The ability of the person to* **survive** *is a factor.*

## Definition of States Requiring Intervention

Using the above examples a person with mental illness warranting treatment in hospital can be defined as someone who:

- acts in a manner not befitting the place
- demonstrates disturbing behaviour over time
- creates an adverse reaction on others
- appears incapable of looking after him/her self

In fact these are the parameters defined by the now defunct Mental Health Act 1983.

Look at the diagram following. I describe an image several people experience. Although the answers are not definitive I hope this offers some insight into the difficulties of separating culture, belief, personal life circumstances and character from diagnosis.

There are a whole spectrum of mental conditions running through that invisible pole which takes us between normality and insanity. We move back and forward along this line all our lives. It is as well to remember that before making judgment on any aspect of mental illness.

See diagram overleaf

## DIFFICULTIES OF DIAGNOSIS

psychotic          spiritual

creative     **?**     'normal'

imaginative  ■   eccentric

*Apply a label to each person using each label once. The contextual explanations are at the bottom of this diagram.*

| | |
|---|---|
| Andrew | Virgin Mary was watching TV in my room. |
| Maureen | Virgin Mary said "happy birthday!" to me. |
| John | Virgin Mary disguises herself as a nun. |
| Stella | I saw someone dressed like Virgin Mary. |
| Giovanni | I paint my vision of Virgin Mary. |
| Bernie | Virgin Mary appeared to me in a cave. |

### CONTEXTUAL EXPLANATIONS

| Label | | Contextual Explanation |
|---|---|---|
| Andrew | PSYCHOTIC | -hallucinating |
| Maureen | IMAGINATIVE | - a normal child |
| John | ECCENTRIC | - eccentric though |
| Stella | NORMAL | — sees an actress |
| Giovanni | CREATIVE | - paints frescos. |
| Bernie | SPIRITUAL | -Catholic saint Bernadette |

## Drawing the line - Sanity and Insanity

Some Psychiatrists notably R D Laing questioned whether mental illness might be a social construct. Philosopher George Berkeley (1685-1753) posed an interesting question; if no one hears the sound of a tree falling in the forest does that sound exist? In terms of mental illness - does insanity exist if there is no one to observe it? Let us consider a metaphor.

- *If a man living alone on an island became psychotic could his extraordinary perceptions be considered sane?*

- *If someone with different perceptions joins him on the island, who is sane and who deluded or are both realities sane or insane?*

- *How many people have to live on the island before one reality is accepted and thereby defines sanity?*

It is possible to define insanity as extraordinary perceptions which other people do not share. *'Extraordinary perception'* is a less prejudicial expression for what has been called insanity or madness. If all extraordinary behaviour were classed as insanity then the religious experiences of hermits and saints would be interpreted as symptoms of madness and not divine inspiration. But if you suggested to a spiritual person their vision was merely a hallucination and should be treated with Haloperidol you would certainly offend them.

If a scientist believes eternal life to be not only possible but has a plan to advance this reality this belief may be thought eccentric but does not make this person insane. The scientist I refer to is Dr Aubrey de Grey, an intelligent computer expert who has been offered a large grant to research his fancy - so evidently someone takes him seriously. So perhaps insanity is also to do with levels of tolerance and knowledge.

In conclusion, culture has a strong influence in defining the reality we live in. Much of what might appear strange is not always the problem of the individual but can be the perception of vociferous others. Stigmatisation, labelling, blaming are often the result of moral panics without cause. However, such negative traits are part of the same binding forces which draw together members of a community at times of perceived attack. Although it is known that mental illness can be made worse by community living it can also be the root of healing. Understanding, harmony and creative activity stabilizes individuals and enables full lives.

# Chapter 2

## Mental Health and Communities

**Content of this Chapter:**
Education
East and West
Evidence Based Treatments
Stress of Living in Communities
Four Community Scenarios

*'Between January 1940 and September 1942, 70,723 mental patients were gassed, chosen by 9 leading professors of psychiatry and 39 top physicians.'* Roy Porter, 'Madness, A Brief History.'

Faulty genetics, environment and life events are all deemed causal factors of mental illness. So too are the stresses of modern life; relationships, work, major illness and living in communities. Even socially inclined animals have fights not only at breeding time but also during times of stress for the pack.

For the human animal, life in communities involves a greater sense of tolerance, forgiveness, understanding and caring than most people are prepared to give and there is a varying capacity for these traits in the first place.

It is human nature to be suspicious of those who are different. This is inbred from our animal origins. What is shocking is when those you least expect it act in that manner. That is the point Roy Porter was making (*epigram above*). Take any community, add a drop of stress and a scattering of malicious gossips and you have a breeding ground for scapegoating.

Prolific serial killer in the UK, Harold Shipman spoke publicly against unkindness toward mental health patients. A so-called normal citizen threatened to shoot a young mental patient who was about to be housed next door to him.

*Imagine what it might be like to suffer delusions and persecutory voices. As you recover and become lucid you realize those around you are mocking or not sympathetic. Do you think this might worsen your illness?*

### Education

Early attitudes developed because the fickle public tended to think of mental illness only when reading sensational headlines. This gave mentally ill people a negative image. For many years the Royal College of Psychiatry liaised with the press to reduce sensationalist headlines in news connected with mental illness.

Educational programmes are carried out in schools, and the public is better informed than in the days of the Care in the Community Act. However those with active mental illness rarely receive the empathy given cancer victims, children's diseases or Aids.

There is a commonly believed stigma that mental illness is the fault of the sufferer. The days when someone with depression is told '*pull yourself together*' or that depression is a kind of moral weakness is not yet over but as diagnosed cases rise this attitude is starting to change.

To conclude, better education about mental illness, the work of mental health charities, publications, negotiations with the media over reducing sensationalist headlines, an increasing tendency to present mental illness sympathetically on television, film and radio and lastly recognition of the fact that mental illness can happen to anyone have lead to a generally more enlightened attitude in the western world in recent times.

## East and West

Cultural factors are also important. Western medicine is different to Chinese medicine. Eastern cultures add current knowledge to past experience rather than replace old with new as we do in the West. Eastern medicine is steeped in tradition whilst in the West sweeping changes come with the latest discovery or new fads. Eastern medicine is inextricably linked to spirituality in a way which is becoming adopted in the West. Whereas Church and belief had become almost defunct after the Victorian age, in other cultures it has continued to be a bedrock to millions for whom spirituality, daily life, food, exercise and herbal medicine are inextricably linked.

The current Western penchant for holistic therapies borrows much from Eastern traditions offering patients access to a richer mix of therapies than would otherwise be available.

## Evidence Based Treatments

The danger of the demand for evidence-based treatment threatens this mix. Though evidence-based medicine prevents quackery it can also limit diversity. Few complementary therapies have been through the rigorous system of Government body NICE (National Institute for Clinical Excellence) whose remit is to test medical interventions.

Although laboratory evidence is vital for synthesized pharmaceutical drugs and botanicals (herbal medicines) which have a strong effect on the nervous system, a relaxed approach might be extended to those alternative therapies with anecdotal evidence of effectiveness. As a case in point acupuncturists and chiropractors have recently been deemed acceptable by the medical establishment.

Spiritual and non-medical treatments can be researched through social (qualitative) methods which allow for reported or anecdotal evidence. There is accepted evidence of the placebo effect (where Doctors successfully treat anxious patients with inert drugs) having positive effect. There is also accepted evidence of *bedside manner* having a part in successful treatment.

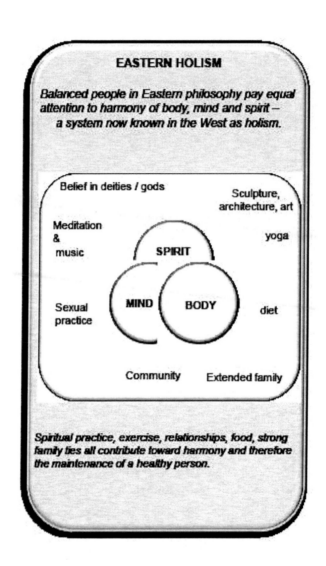

Some years ago a television documentary by scientist Professor Cathy Sykes of the University of Bristol enquired into the effectiveness of alternative medicines including healing and acupuncture. Dr Sykes holds the Collier Chair in Public Understanding of Science and is colloquially known as the people's scientist. Dr Sykes wants current opposition between medicine and alternative therapies to be bridged.

In a BBC documentary series *Alternative Medicine: The Evidence* she investigated acupuncture, spiritual healing and meditation. Although her views are opposed by some of the scientific fraternity Dr Sykes believes there is much to be learned. For example she discussed links between placebo and faith with regard to spiritual healing.

Among Professor Sykes' conclusions was that the brain is more plastic than scientists initially thought. scientists have proved that inserting needles in certain acupuncture points has a marked effect on the area of the brain dealing with the perception of pain.

No one knows how ECT works neither is there clinical evidence for a huge number of botanic materials used effectively as medications for centuries, some of which have been synthesized as pharmaceutical drugs and many others of which are under current investigation.

Bringing scientific principles to untapped areas of treatment can only be to the good of those concerned. One must balance this with anecdotal evidence of success but also the knowledge of charlatanism for personal gain.

## Stress of Living in Communities

Living in communities can be a stressful experience with its indignities, errors of understanding and rebuttals. What we call bullying is known to result in psychiatric injury often requiring long-term treatment. Why does this behaviour result in such damage? It is because we are social creatures and enforced isolation is against our nature.

Cruel experiments were carried out on young chimpanzees in the 1950's. Some unfortunate creatures were deprived of their mothers and became distressed, some of them dying, proving social shock can cause devastation to the nervous system.

In totalitarian states isolation is used as a method of torture. Solitary confinement with enforced psychiatric medication can lead to mental illness. If exiles are returned to their communities they suffer extreme anxiety, mistrust and negative symptoms which may last a lifetime. Russian poet Marina Tsvetaeva hanged herself after being isolated for years in appalling conditions in the Russian Gulag, her daughter, sister and husband all imprisoned. On the other side are those born into loving families with friends and careers yet succumb to suicide.

Mental suffering is insidious because it can neither be perceived by the self or others in the way physical hurts can. Sometimes suffering is so hidden under smiles, success, perfect family and other covers it goes undiscovered and ends in suicide. There is nothing anyone can do in such circumstances. After a suicide in a family it is always difficult to alleviate the mixed feelings of anger, grief, guilt and blame.

Mental illness can become so intractable it is difficult to treat. As well as individual and family support, mental wellbeing is connected with living in a positive community and a feeling of belonging. I offer four examples which demonstrate this theme.

## Four Community Scenarios

Consider what would happen in your community:

- A woman experiences people whom no one else sees or hears.
- A man mutters to himself scratching his head until it bleeds.
- A female child is heard to scream and cry every night

See diagram overleaf.

## SOCIAL PROBLEMS -
### of long term mental illness

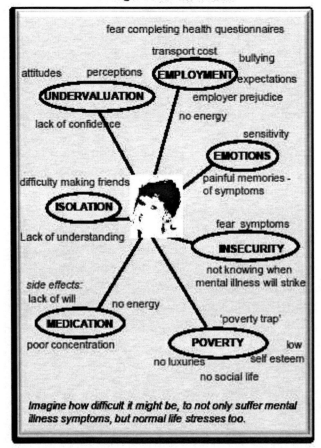

fear completing health questionnaires

transport cost

bullying

attitudes    perceptions    **EMPLOYMENT** expectations

**UNDERVALUATION**    employer prejudice

lack of confidence    no energy

sensitivity

**EMOTIONS**

difficulty making friends    painful memories - of symptoms

**ISOLATION**

fear symptoms

Lack of understanding

**INSECURITY**

not knowing when mental illness will strike

side effects: lack of will    no energy

**MEDICATION**    'poverty trap'

poor concentration    **POVERTY**    low

no luxuries    self esteem

no social life

*Imagine how difficult it might be, to not only suffer mental illness symptoms, but normal life stresses too.*

In community A all are recognized as behaving oddly but the community is compassionate. The woman is sent for observation to a psychiatric hospital. The man is offered social support and treatment. The child is taken into care after it is discovered that her parents have been abusing her.

In community B where ancestors are revered, all three are looked upon with awe, as they are believed to be infused with the spirits of deceased tribe members. The individuals are treated well. Their families are given gifts. The community would be outraged if it was suggested any of the three were mentally ill.

In community C people are afraid of strange behaviour which is believed to stem from bad spirits. The woman is hanged, the man exiled, the child is tortured then murdered.

In community D there is a history of violence and crime. The three go unnoticed. The woman becomes ill and stabs a man under the delusion he is attacking her. The man is followed by a gang of youths who taunt him. He commits suicide. The child is repeatedly hit by her parents. She runs away and is found wandering by a pimp (someone who lives off the earnings of prostitutes). He drugs her then forces her into prostitution. She is found unconscious in a squalid bedsit, a dirty syringe by her side.

Although the characters are fictitious I have described real life circumstances. Sometimes it is not a matter of where you live but the circle of people you are born into which determine your fate.

If you can cope with difficult subject matter read the Victoria Climbie Enquiry which details the horrific murder of a small child whose relatives believed she was a witch. More horrific is the fact her murder took place not in a remote part of the third world but in London.

## CULTURE AND DIAGNOSIS

*What is perceived as mental illness only has meaning within the context of the culture it occurs in. Consider the examples below:*

| | |
|---|---|
| **1. Woman** | **has visual & auditory hallucinations** |
| **2. Man** | **a solitary who mutters to himself** |
| **3. Child** | **shouts, screams and is destructive** |

*Treatment:*

**COMMUNITY A (tolerant)**
*Sent for assessment*

**COMMUNITY B (ancestor worship)**
*Revered. Their families are given gifts.*

**COMMUNITY C (staid, enclosed culture)**
*All are shunned as a result of fear among the members of the community*

**COMMUNITY D (violent / criminal)**
*'Every man for himself'. Left to cope in a harsh environment, symptoms worsen until untreatable.*

*Psychologists believe individuals are responsible for their own destiny. In caring communities we have to accept the part we play in individual's difficulties. The first (blame) view excuses bullying and scape-goating.*

31

# Chapter 3

## A Brief History of Mental Illness to the 17<sup>th</sup> Century

---

**Content of this Chapter:**
Primitive Beliefs
Ancient Civilizations [myths]
Hippocrates and Medical Reasoning
Other Ancient Treatments
Medieval Belief
16<sup>th</sup> Century – Change of Attitude
Bethlem Asylum –Medieval to 17<sup>th</sup> Century

Beliefs about the cause of mental illness have a strong bearing on how that illness is perceived and treated. The examples of the four communities in the previous chapter demonstrate this. It is an interesting exercise to look through history and compare our ancestors' attitudes with that of today.

You will find many books on the market on the history of mental illness but I particularly recommend Roy Porter whose book I have listed in the further resources section.

### Primitive Beliefs

Although no one knows for certain the thought processes of early man, archaeologists make educated guesses through examining artifacts and structures at gravesites, comparing them with similar sites across the world. For example it is commonly accepted that primitive people drew pictures on cave walls as an act of faith, believing they were creating the right conditions for successful hunting expeditions.

Many sacrificial victims have been found where the victim had been either hanged or bludgeoned with an axe. Although most Western peoples find sacrifice abhorrent it is necessary to understand terror in primitive minds about the caprices of nature. Storms, eclipses and the passing of the sun across the sky each day were feared because the primitive mind had no way of telling if or when these would pass. If you were facing violent unknown forces it might seem obvious to assume such forces were created by powerful beings needing appeasement.

## Historic Trepanning

There is evidence of crude brain surgery from 40,000 years ago. A circular hole was cut into the skull presumably to let out evil spirits. This occurred in many cultures throughout the Stone Age, Ancient Greece and Rome. Skulls have been found with trepanned holes and surprisingly there is evidence of bone growth around the holes, proving many people survived.

Trepanning is still used, albeit rarely, to relieve pressure on the brain in the case of wounds to the head. Small holes are drilled by surgeons to give pressure relief between brain and skull.

## Ancient Civilizations

Man began worshipping gods when afflictions of mind and body were attributed as punishment sent by angry gods. A priest offered prayers or sacrifices to appease the deity in the hope of staving off further punishment. Priests were the forerunners of doctors and held powerful positions in their community. Mere kings took political rule by force of arms but deities were capable of destroying human lives.

The Greeks believed gods punished those who opposed them by giving them impossible moral tasks. This is a brief example of such a moral dilemma in a simplified version of the Greek myth of the House of Agamemnon. When you read it, remember these two ancient Greek truths:

- Disobeying a god is a sin punishable by the Furies
- Matricide (killing a mother) is a sin punishable by death

### Myth of the House of Agamemnon

*The god Apollo orders Orestes, son of King Agamemnon & Queen Clytemnestra, to put his mother to death because she and her lover had murdered her husband.*

*Orestes agonises over the god's direction. If he kills Clytemnestra he will disobey the law of goddess Athena (that matricide is punishable by death). If he does not, he will be disobeying Apollo's orders and will be hounded by the Furies.*

*Orestes helped by his sister Elektra kills Clytemnestra and her lover Aegisthus. Orestes is inflicted with madness by the Furies.*

*Just as Orestes is nearing the point of death Athena intervenes and the curse of the House of Agamemnon is lifted.*

The Greeks were fond of moral dilemmas which were plays with masked players and a Chorus of actors who spoke the voice of conscience. None of these dramas or Tragedies ends happily. The hero or heroine inevitably dies or is sent mad. It is the ancient equivalent of The Terminator.

Centuries before Sigmund Freud, the Greeks recognized how moral dilemmas (what we might call mental conflict) could result in loss of reason. Once these conflicts had been worked through the sufferer was cleansed and might recover. This is not too far away from Freudian thinking or modern drama therapy.

When animal sacrifices or moral retribution no longer seemed enough to appease unhappy and vindictive gods, hey presto the scapegoat was invented. Scapegoats could represent individuals, tribes or larger communities. The scapegoat could be animal or human or for greater effect both, and had two purposes;

- to appease the deity so that the intended victim got off
- to provide the deity with a gift

35

## SCAPEGOAT SYSTEM

*The scapegoat is a personalised concept of sacrifice for early humans, who imagined that gods controlled both man and nature.*

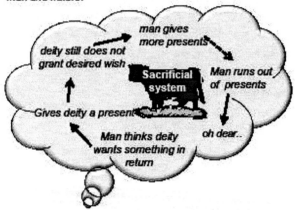

**Deity withholds something man wants or needs.**

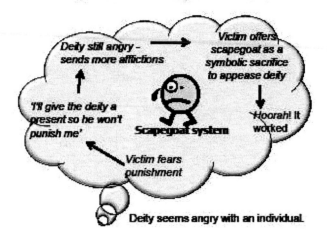

**Deity seems angry with an individual.**

This triangle of perceived sin, punishment and sacrifice can be understood as antecedents of modern moral panics. there are examples on varying scales common throughout history:

*A murder is committed. An eccentric individual [guilty or not] is blamed and his sacrificial lambasting in newspapers eases the fear of the rest of the community until the real culprit is caught.*

*In large organizations, changes that affect existing staff are disliked but staff are afraid to express opposition because they do not want to be seen as trouble makers. There is a tense atmosphere and 'elephants in the room'. Someone who does not fit in is blamed for all the ensuing problems and is ejected. Those who threw spanners in the works experience the double delight of committing mischief and getting someone else blamed.*

## Hippocrates and Medical Reasoning

Hippocrates was a Greek philosopher highly regarded in his day and now credited as the father of modern medicine. He made a study of illnesses of the mind two thousand years ahead of his time. Hippocrates disagreed with conventional views and concluded madness was '*No more divine nor sacred than other diseases but has a natural cause.*'

Hippocrates was the first to overturn the conventional view of madness as punishment by gods. Pre-empting modern medical science he noted through examination of patients and careful observations three different types of mental disorder:

- Brain fever
- Mania
- Melancholia

These terms would have been familiar in the nineteenth century indeed the term 'mania' is still in use. Shakespeare's play Hamlet contains what is considered an accurate description of melancholia or what is now called depressive illness.

Hippocrates, Galen and their followers made a study of the four humors or vital fluids of the body. When these humors became unbalanced, illness resulted. This system is closely allied with the holistic beliefs of Chinese medicine and Western alternative therapies. There is also a parallel in that Psychiatrists believe mental illness such as depression to be caused by an imbalance in natural brain chemicals.

I have depicted this crossover of early medicine, science, philosophy and nature in the schematic diagram on the next page in the form of a Mandela. Mandelas represent balancing forces and are used in magic rituals.

Starting from the outer circle are:

- **alchemy** - elemental symbols air, earth, fire, water
- **seasons** – each fixed with certain religious rites
- **physical states** - caused by imbalance of humors
- **humors** – vital body fluids

The sixteenth century patient would have been treated by an Apothecary in order to have their humors balanced and remain in good health. This was achieved by:

- purging – through inducing vomiting
- bloodletting - using lancets or leeches

Unfortunately purging often killed already weak patients as did the application of leeches and bleeding.

In a retrospective, 21$^{st}$ century surgeons are using leeches to clean infected wounds and finding them more effective and less harmful than strong medications which would be otherwise used. Leeches secrete a solution which prevents the blood from clotting and can be coaxed into difficult-to-reach areas of the human body.

## Mandela

This diagram demonstrates wholeness, using ideas from medicine, philosophy and science. Circular symmetries or mandelas were thought to have magical, spiritual and healing properties. Philosophers, in their role as the first scientists discovered all kinds of symmetries in nature, phenomena & man.

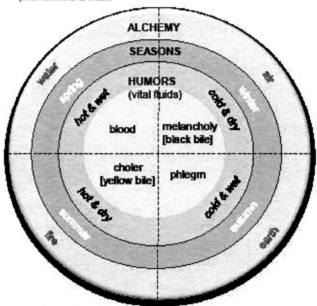

## Other Ancient Treatments

The Greek philosopher Plato said *madmen* (his term) ought to be locked away at home. In fact, this practice was widespread until the early nineteenth century. Romans were familiar with and tolerant of depressive illness. They treated it with warm baths, music and well-lit rooms. Such treatments would be beneficial.

Greeks and Romans had access to sleep temples where soporific herbs were given as curative aids to rest and sleep. In modern times a form of sleep treatment called *modified narcosis* was used with depressed patients suffering exhaustion through lack of sleep. The narcosis was induced by drugs.

Romans also reportedly used electric eels to shock patients out of madness. In 19th century Bethlem Hospital, patients were lowered into a tub of eels for the same purpose. This curious treatment may be a precursor of 20th century electric shock treatment (ECT).

## Medieval Belief

By medieval times there seems to have been a mix between divine retribution, witchcraft and a more enlightened attitude towards the examination and legal treatment of *idiots* and *lunatics*. These historic terms did not have the prejudicial connotation they have today. The term idiot meant born defective and lunatic meant afflicted by the actions of the moon. Both conditions were treated with the same regime.

The common belief in witchcraft lasted until late into the 17th century. Sick people and animals were believed possessed by evil spirits as a result of curses made by witches (human servants of the devil). The Church, concerned at immoral sexual activity between monks and nuns blamed the Devil for inciting them to passion. The book *The Devils of Loudun* by Aldous Huxley (and film of the same name directed by Ken Russell) is a graphic depiction of this time in history.

In contrast to the dark side of medieval beliefs there is a very interesting article by David and Christine Roffe in the British Medical Journal concerning Emma de Beston.

De Beston's case is one of few surviving accounts depicting a medieval woman brought before a local Inquisition for lunacy. The woman was treated fairly by the Inquisition despite the wicked intent of those trying to deprive her of liberty and her property. Although she never recovered her reason the Inquisition enabled her to regain her property and access welfare services.

This unusual case is a model of fairness which Roffe interestingly compares with less favourable patient experiences during the Care in the Community Act (1990's). However it was not all enlightenment and fairness at this time.

## Bethlehem Hospital

Bethlem or Bedlam was an insane Asylum set up through public subscription in 1377. It was on the site of a much earlier Priory, the Church of St Mary of Bethlehem, after which it was named. The first mentally ill patients here were recorded in 1403 when it also housed poor and physically ill patients.

Private *madhouses* also existed at this time but were run as businesses. Wealthy patients paid for their keep whilst the poor had their accommodation paid by the Parish. It had been common for the insane to be prosecuted and imprisoned for bizarre or anti-social manner and Bethlem became an alternative to prison.

Bethlem's purpose was to lock up the insane out of harm's way; more pertinently out of sight of their families and society. In effect these places became dumping grounds for unwanted relatives and misfits. It contained a mix of patients because in this age there were no distinctions between physical and mental illnesses nor what we might distinguish social and forensic [criminal] problems. An Asylum might contain people with:

- Organic brain disease – epilepsy - cerebral palsy
- injuries to the brain - head injuries
- socially unacceptable - prostitutes, thieves and beggars

## 16ᵗʰ Century – Change of Attitude

By the 16th Century mental illness was viewed as illness or malady rather than divine punishment. Roy Porter describes the changes towards a more philosophical view and quotes the Philosopher Descartes *'reason can rescue man from insanity'*.

Freed from ancient beliefs of divine retribution, nevertheless becoming mad continued to be regarded as a curse inflicted by the Devil which could be cured only through prayer and bible reading. This view conveniently aided the church in maintaining power over frightened communities.

Later, monasteries and nunneries started providing shelter for the insane within the grounds of their communities where inmates were tolerated and treated kindly.

## New For Old – Lazar Houses Revamped as Asylums

In his excellent book *Madness and Civilization* (written in the 1960's) Michel Foucault makes interesting parallels between religious fervour and the exclusion of those perceived as sinners.

Leprosy had been a scourge from the Middle Ages and thousands of Lazar Houses had been set up where lepers could find refuge after being forcibly excluded from their communities. Popular belief dictated that leprosy was a punishment for sins and to cast out a leper was an act of religious piety. As Foucault ironically remarks *'the sinner who abandons the leper at his door opens his [the sinner's] way to heaven'*.

By the 16th Century this policy of social exclusion had one benefit. By separating lepers from society the spread of leprosy reduced as the disease is spread through skin contact.

By the end of the century Lazar Houses were virtually empty. These crumbling buildings scattered throughout Europe were used to isolate all those considered outcasts by virtue of their mental state (wanderers, vagabonds, the insane and anyone not considered fit to enter civilized society).

## Ship of Fools

Alongside forcibly stuffing the insane into ex-Lazar Houses the citizens found another convenient way of tidying their streets. There was a supposed affinity between calmness and the sea and it was believed the sea would cure mad minds. Foucault describes how madmen would be given into the care of mariners who took them on long voyages. These voyages were on trade ships.

In effect these lunatic travelers often did get better through improved environmental conditions, removal from public humiliation, fresh air, fresh food and calm. In mental illness excess stimuli (noise, confusion, lack of routine) are generally counter-productive to creating the calm required for confused minds to recover.

The other side of the coin were lonely deaths far from their native country. One wonders how many died at sea or were put over the side if the mariners could not cope with bizarre behaviour. Casting overboard ill human cargo was common during the slave trade. Ship of Fools became an allegorical term with both romantic and macabre aspects and is written into folklore and art. Read Foucault's splendid book for more detail.

## Bethlem Asylum – Medieval to 17th Century

In early times, treatments were crude and would now be looked on as inhumane. However, we have to realize that mental illness has only relatively recently been recognized as needing treatment as much as physical ailments.

It is ironical that, whilst the ancient Romans provided Temples of Sleep with light and air for those in mental turmoil in the seventeenth century such wretches were incarcerated in Asylums. Their symptoms were feared or laughed at and the prevailing attitude was '*cast them out of society*'. They were believed incurable. When Bethlem Hospital was built, no one who entered was expected to recover – most would die within the walls, some after decades of malnourishment and maltreatment.

Male and female patients were kept in appalling conditions, naked, restrained or chained, sleeping on straw bedding. Vomiting and purging were common treatments thought to reduce a patient's strength and keep them under control.

Other treatments consisted of vomiting and purging to weaken the patients and lessen any potential violence. It was considered wasteful to give out too much food in view of the nature of the treatment. Following are other barbaric treatments administered at Bethlem. I have indicated in *italics* how 17th century doctors believed they worked:

- put in a tub with electric eels [*shock them to wellness*]
- drawing blood [*excess blood causes madness*]
- lowered in water inside a box with holes [*fear forced a patient to sanity*]
- spinning patient on a stool [*shaking the brain into sanity*]
- cutting off the clitoris [*sexual organs caused melancholia*]

Doctors in this establishment formulated their own medicines with none of the controls which exist today. Patients were forced to pay for their medication, giving the Doctors handsome profits.

On Sundays the public could pay one penny to view patients as a kind of entertainment but serious visitors interested in patient welfare were discouraged. Thankfully in 1770 this noxious practice was banned. If you cannot imagine this scenario look at 17th century artist William Hogarth's series of drawings *The Rake's Progress* where fictional *Tom Rakewell* descends into madness and is imprisoned in Bethlem.

Occasionally patients were discharged and given a badge as a license to beg in the surrounding villages. In a cruel reversal they were expected to repay the cost of their treatment in Bethlem out of their meagre earnings. As a matter of interest, Bethlem hospital is still open and has a museum containing the art of mentally ill people from Victorian times to the present and is open to the public on certain days.

# Chapter 4

## Mental Illness 18th - 20th Century

---

**Content of this Chapter:**
The York Retreat 1796
Degeneration (Benedict Morel 1809 – 1873)
Asylums after 1820
Victorian Poets and Fashionable Melancholia
Psychosurgery
Hypnosis, Regression & Psychological Approaches
Behaviourists
Asylums in the 20th Century
1960's – 1970's Encounter Groups
Cognitive Behavioural Therapies
Milton Erickson 1970's
2000 Anti Psychiatric Movement: Szaz & Laing
Dialectical Behaviour Therapy (DBT)
21st Century - Ongoing Knowledge

By the early eighteenth century madness was commonly viewed as a disease of the mind. In 1788 King George III was diagnosed with mental illness and received therapy at his home. Doctors variously treated him with antimony (containing arsenic) and being chained in a straightjacket every time he had an episode of madness, an early form of behavioural therapy.

The King is now believed to have contracted porphyria through ingestion of the arsenic used to powder his wigs and from medication containing arsenic which his doctors prescribed.

Doctors started to explore links between the nervous system, senses and intellect. Studies were made of shaking palsy (epilepsy), tics, hallucinations and aphasia (disturbance of the senses).

Two anatomists invented Phrenology, a study of the personality by examining contours of the brain which was briefly popular before being discredited as unscientific.

### The York Retreat 1796

In 1796 The Quaker William Tuke set up an institution based on moral therapy where patients lived-in with staff. Tuke had witnessed a fellow Quaker dying in an Asylum and was determined no one else should suffer in such a way. His patients were rewarded for good behaviour and punished for bad in the hope this type of moral / bible therapy would restore their minds.

The Retreat is still active though not in its original form. It was a forerunner of modern sanctuaries such as Maytree in London where suicidal patients stay for a maximum of four days, an opportunity for retreat in a friendly environment with access to therapists.

### Degeneration (Benedict Morel 1809 – 1873)

Morel's theory of degeneration might be perceived as a forerunner of theories that lead to discovery of genes. Morel believed family characteristics were passed through generations through birth defects. Morel outlined the stages as:

1. Alcohol and opiate addiction
2. Prostitution and sexual degeneracy
3. Criminality
4. Insanity
5. Imbecility
6. Sterility [end of the family]

*Imbecility* was one of a number of historic terms used to describe what we now call people with learning disabilities.

Morel thought degeneracy [reversal] had its initial cause in drug or alcohol abuse or diseases like malaria or moral sickness. He was convinced diseased families would become sterile and die out naturally. His beliefs might be paralleled with Darwin's early theories of natural selection and the quasi science of eugenics so disastrously taken up by Adolf Hitler.

## Asylums after 1820

Victorian Asylums held up to 1000 patients in what resembled mini-towns. Acres of land surrounding Asylums contained kitchens, chapels, laundries, industrial units and kitchen gardens. Patients were expected to take up a trade such as shoe making, laundry work or gardening and were expected to work as hard as their peers in the infamous Workhouses.

Asylums were not seen as places for recuperation but as houses of correction for moral regeneration and work. The saving grace was their location in the countryside with access to fresh air, fresh vegetables and away from mocking townsfolk.

An 1820 Act of Parliament made it compulsory to have medically qualified practitioners in attendance at Asylums. Previously they were administered by Superintendents who whilst not medically qualified were experienced in dealing with inmate behaviour. One might parallel such officers with 1990's Rehabilitation staff who cared for ex-Asylum patients.

By 1845 every county had to build an Asylum and by 1890 two medical certificates had to be signed before anyone could be detained. These measures were brought in to stem cruel practices like dumping socially-difficult relatives (*moral defectives*) in Asylums when these people had no symptoms of mental illness. There were also those who sought early inheritance by locking unwanted relatives away for life.

Many Victorian creatives were incarcerated in such places including artist Richard Dadd and poet William Cowper. Rich patients were usually treated either in private madhouses run by Doctors or in their own homes.

Reformer Robert Gardiner Hill ran the Lincoln Asylum where restraints and strait jackets were replaced with activity-centred therapy, a wholesome diet and exercise. Art therapies were available to patients and these remain popular today. Not surprisingly this regime proved successful.

If you want to see what Asylums look like try your local Records Office. My photographs of St John's Hospital, Stone, near Aylesbury, Buckinghamshire are held in the archives of the *Centre for Buckinghamshire Studies.*

## Victorian Poets and Fashionable Melancholia

By Late Victorian times being *melancholy* had become fashionable in artistic circles and among the public who adored them. Victorians created an enduring romantic image of pale and languid artistic types sitting among idyllic sylvan scenes whilst partaking of *laudanum* (opium) to enhance their writings. Keats, Shelley, Byron, Dickens, Coleridge and abolitionist William Wilberforce all partook of this dangerous and addictive drug. The '*mildly mad*' popular Victorian image was attached to Lord Byron who was famously referred to by his lover as '*mad, bad and dangerous to know*'.

The truth was less delightful. There were frequent deaths from the arsenic or laudanum taken to get the popular '*tuberculosis look*' of pallid flesh and large eyes, somewhat similar to the look adopted by 21$^{st}$ century *Goths*. The melancholia exhibited by these socialites was far from the somber truth of depressive illness with its lethal suicidal urges.

## Psychosurgery
## Phineas Gage

In 1848 an event took place which was to radically alter the treatment of behaviour disorders.

Railroad worker Phineas Gage was exploding rocks with dynamite. A charge went off accidentally and drove a long 25mm diameter steel rod up into his brain through one of his eyes. Immediately after his horrific accident Gage became unconscious and had fits. Gage was studied by many eminent doctors of the day. Although he survived 11 years after the accident he became aggressive to an extent that his friends said they no longer recognised him. Gage died of a series of seizures nearly a decade after his accident.

Gage's skull is now kept in the Warren Anatomical Museum of Harvard Medical School. Recently, photographs have been found of Gage and these can be viewed online. Gage's brain was examined by many scientists over the years. As a result of this long research it became possible to pinpoint the different brain areas responsible for personality and mood.

## Pre-Frontal Leucotomy

The first modern brain surgery came about as a result of the research on Gage. Surgeons experimented with a procedure called lobotomy (or leucotomy), severing the frontal lobes from the brain which it was hoped would cure a range of serious problems; severe behaviour problems, schizophrenia and depression which did not respond to other treatment.

The first lobotomy was carried out by Egas Moniz in 1935 who won the 1949 Nobel Prize for his work. As a footnote I gather he was shot dead by a patient he had lobotomised.

Psychiatrist Walter Freeman carried out over 2000 lobotomy operations, using an ice pick which he swept under the brow-ridge of his patients to cut the frontal lobes. Some 50,000 patients underwent operations in the 1950's of whom 10% died.

This crude surgery was always controversial even among Psychiatrists, who felt that to interfere with personality through surgery was unethical. These operations had a negative effect on personality, mood and social functioning and were irreversible. Such operations were discontinued in 1975.

## Hypnosis, Regression & Psychological Approaches
### Charcot [1835 - 1893] & Breuer [1842 - 1925]

Hypnotherapy is the grandfather of all Psychotherapies. Jean Martin Charcot worked extensively with patients diagnosed with hysterical paralyses of limb or voice, now called conversion disorders (para*lyses as a result of psychological trauma*). Conversion disorders were common in the early eighteenth century but are less frequent now.

Charcot discovered a deep form of relaxation he termed *hypnosis* and used *hypnotic suggestion* to successfully free his patients from physical symptoms. Charcot did not know how this worked, just that it did.

Following on from this work Charcot's colleague Joseph Breuer allowed patients to talk under hypnosis. The term *talking cure* was coined by one of Breuer's celebrated cases Anna O, who used it to describe how she was freed from neurotic symptoms after being hypnotised.

### Sigmund Freud [1856 1939]

Freud was a devotee of Charcot and Breuer and collaborated with both during his early career. Breuer and Freud collaborated to coin a new term *catharsis* (Greek for cleansing or discharging) to describe the process of treatment.

It was Freud who first started asking questions about how this treatment worked and developed his theories of *mind* after years of studying patients. The location of mind, a function of the brain, is still unknown. It is unfortunate that whilst Freud became famous the pioneering work of Charcot and Breuer became largely forgotten.

Psychoanalysis was Freud's development from hypnosis. His life work was studying the hidden world of mind or subconscious. Freud realized it was not the hypnotic state which was responsible for cure but a therapeutic relationship between doctor and patient. He discarded hypnosis and allowed the patient to talk freely in the conscious state.

Freud used dream analysis to gain access to the subconscious. Freud called dreams '*the royal road to the unconscious*'; that is, the most direct route to understanding the unconscious mind. He studied symbolic meaning in dreams and helped patients interpret their own dreams. Another method Freud used was free association.
    The patient was encouraged to say anything which came into their mind. This, he believed, triggered hidden memories which had been repressed by the conscious mind. Freud helped patients interpret the results. Through re-visiting, thus gaining insight (understanding) into painful earlier experiences, Freud's patients became psychologically healthier and had better relationships.

A great deal of negative publicity surrounded Freud's early theory that children repressed sexual interest in their parents. When he heard children complaining they had been raped by a parent, he thought this to be the result of infantile fantasies rather than the truth. His thinking ran along the lines; children only matured when they were able to accept they could not have a sexual relationship with their parent. He believed *rape fantasy* was an expression of this unconscious wish.

Certainly the rape fantasy theory negatively affected children who had been raped by a parent and were not believed and this error persisted for years. Freud later renounced this theory. However, even this error of judgment cannot negate the massive contribution Freud made to understanding the nature of mind.

Freud and his follower Carl Jung are now considered the founding fathers of psychological therapies.

## Carl Jung [1875 - 1961] - Analytical Psychology

Jung was initially a devotee of Freud. Freud expected Jung to become his heir, continuing to support psychoanalytic theory. But that was not to be. Jung began to have doubts and eventually split with his former mentor.

Jung was deeply interested in philosophy and studied world mythology, spiritual and religious beliefs. He studied the Pueblo-Indian tribe who believed their rituals made the sun move around the sky and ensured the continuity of the seasons. This belief that they were integral to the cycle of existence gave Pueblo Indians inner confidence. Jung concluded that it was essential for men to have a spiritual dimension to their life.

From his study of world mythology Jung discovered links between cultures and across the generations. Common character types from myths were the hero, the wise man and the fool; this is the hero, for example:

*a man is born of a virgin and is then sacrificed. Later he is resurrected and comes back to save his people.*

*See diagram overleaf.*

## CONSCIOUS & UNCONSCIOUS MIND
### how we process experience

4) - output thinking [conscious]
We form conclusions about experiences from the products of 1, 2 & 3 - sensory input, comparison with past experience AND collective memories from our ancestry. This processing determines if the current event (new experience) is viewed in a negative or positive way.

1) - input via the senses:
[conscious]
We experience events through the senses [sight, touch, taste, hearing, smell]. These are processed in short term memory.

2) - comparison
[unconscious]
The event is filtered to a part of memory where it is compared with past experience.

3) The Collective Unconscious
The part of mind apparent in dreams or feelings such as 'Deja-vou' [a sense of experiencing the same event on previous occasions].

Jung's theory of collective unconscious - memories that contain the myths of our ancestors.

Some scientists believe mind exists through all the sensory cells in the body - not only the brain.

If you want to read more I recommend:

- Larousse Book of World Mythology
- Standard Stories from the Opera
- Man and his Symbols (Jung)

Jung deduced that the *personality* is a process of mind and comprises *archetypical* characters which manifest according to the situation. The work of a Jungian Analyst is to assist their patient to integrate their archetypes in a process Jung termed *individuation*.

Jung's studies of archetypes lead to his consideration of some kind of carrier which allowed racial memories to be retained across generations. His solution was *the collective unconscious*. The term *unconscious* refers to the fact that we are unaware of archetypal memories except under certain conditions:

- the symbolism of dreams
- *de ja vue* – an instinct we have experienced something before
- *memories* - unconnected with our personal experience

Déjà vu is an interesting phenomenon which scientists are researching. It may have connections with what is called *false memory syndrome* where people insist they experienced something which could not have happened. An interesting film which demonstrates déjà vu is *Groundhog Day*.

Jung also coined the terms:

- **Introvert** - inner reflective personality
- **Extrovert** - worldly and sociable personality

Jung carried out his studies decades before scientists discovered genes. If you consider his conclusions in this light, the work is remarkable. Sadly he left few books behind to explain how his thinking developed or to integrate all his theories, work which was left to his followers.

Behaviourists

The Behaviourists were psychologists who were looking for rational explanations for human behaviour. Four renowned behaviourists are:

1. Ivan Pavlov [1849 -1936]
2. John Watson [1878-1958]
3. Edward Thorndike [1874-1949]
4. Burrus Skinner [1904 - 1990]

Ivan Pavlov conducted experiments on animal behaviour. Pavlov proved that responses to a stimulus could be changed in animals through a now famous experiment with dogs. Pavlov had a bell rung each time his dogs were given food. Before long the dogs started to salivate as soon as they heard the bell therefore the bell not the food had been the trigger for salivation. Pavlov's collaborator John Watson continued this work discovering human behaviour was not inborn but conditioned [changed] through life experience. The two arguments of Pavlov and Watson are now commonly known as 'nature versus nurture'.

Skinner continued Thorndike's work by placing rats in a maze. The rats were rewarded for going in the right direction or punished by electric shock for going the wrong way. He drew the conclusion that animals and humans learn through reward and punishment. Mental illnesses treated by behavioural therapy at that time included depressive illness, phobias and addictions to drugs and alcohol.

Asylums in the 20th Century

By the late 20th century Asylums still housed very aged patients from the Victorian era, incarcerated virtually all their lives. I met some of the last surviving patients who suffered this cruel method of social injustice. Now in their 80's/90's they lived out their lives in Asylums with few receiving any visitors. One patient was an unmarried mother who was diagnosed as a social misfit. Another had stolen a bicycle when he was a teenager and had been *put away* by his embarrassed parents.

To this sad group were now added a new tranch, those causing difficulties in the community because of mental behavioural problems (before the rise of workable psychiatric medication). They had no alternative treatment other than separation from home and family in an Asylum.

A 1980 expose in the Sun Newspaper and recent Channel 4 documentary revealed how the Queen Mother's cousins Katherine and Nerissa Bowes-Lyon were locked in Asylums as children because they were born with learning disabilities. These children were listed in Burkes Peerage as deceased to avoid embarrassment to the Royal Family. Neither were reputed to have received visits or presents from their illustrious relatives. One died recently, the other is still alive living in an Asylum.

Modern mentally ill individuals were placed in Asylums through the Mental Health Act 1983 legislation, which is the subject of another chapter.

New treatments were by now being introduced including an early form of behavioural therapy called *Token Economy* and newly invented psychiatric drugs like Largactil and Lithium.

Despite the grim Victorian buildings many and varied facilities were set up in the Asylums (now called Psychiatric Hospitals); libraries, shops, occupational therapy units with different kinds of pastimes, canteens and large laundries. Asylums also had a chapel and Chaplain.

Visits to the town for coffee and walks were frequent and considered part of the treatment. Residents of the village seemed tolerant having being used to years of bizarre behaviour. Such behaviour was highly visible, as no anti psychotic drugs existed to alleviate symptoms.

There was a lack of individual care which meant for example patients being dressed from a communal pool of clothing, something which would not occur in our enlightened times. Beds were ranged along each side of a ward housing large numbers of patients with lockers and beds in a large, open plan Ward. Few patients had personal possessions or pictures of family, the whole scenario being institution and functional.

Patients would be woken early for dressing and breakfast before ward round [*when drugs were administered*] and given no choice about having a lie in bed if they chose. The wards were run on authoritarian principles, lead by a Ward Sister. The keynote was efficiency and hygiene the latter bearing more scrutiny than that which appears to exist in general hospitals today.

### 1950's Lithium Valium and Largactil

After the 1950's a drug called lithium was used to treat mania and manic-depressive psychosis. Lithium is a metal salt and was effective in levelling mood but dangerous if overdosed. Patients on this medication had their blood tested regularly by doctors.

Early anti-psychotic drugs such as Largactil were clumsy and became known as *liquid coshes* because they made patients lethargic. In the 1960's the tranquillisers Librium and Valium were prescribed to mainly women for nervous disorders until being withdrawn from use when they were found to be addictive.

Psychiatric medication was at its height throughout these decades up until the 1980's and the brief rise of Prozac. Heralded as the wonder drug and a cure for depression this class of drug (SSRI's) was later damned as a potential causal factor in suicide.

## Token Economy

A 1970's form of behavioural therapy was token economy. Patients were rewarded for good behaviour by being given plastic tokens which they could exchange for cigarettes, cups of tea and treats like biscuits. But human nature always triumphs. What the psychologists on the Ward might not have realized was a black economy in tokens went on late at night after day staff left.

## 1960's – 1970's Encounter Groups

Encounter groups were based on work by Carl Rogers, Fritz Perls and others who had the idealistic aim of improving human potential. In T Groups and later Encounter Groups members were encouraged to discuss their deepest feelings with other members.

However, this was based on a trust system which ultimately did not work because the group leaders were not all they should have been. Vulnerable members of the group were at risk from vociferous others. Encounter Groups are now discredited.

## Cognitive Behavioural Therapies

Cognitive (= *to recognise*) therapists believed that those who consistently experienced frustrations, anxieties and emotional problems in life had faulty patterns of thinking. They attributed these negative thinking patterns to dysfunctional childhood or negative life experience.

Cognitive therapy was a psychological approach which helped patients recognize, challenge and change negative thoughts and their associated negative emotions and behaviour.

Behavioural and cognitive therapies were later combined into cognitive-behavioural therapy (CBT) which remains treatment of choice for psychological elements of mental illnesses.

## Milton Erickson 1970's

In the 1970's Erickson (an American Psychiatrist) pioneered a method which had patients flocking to his clinics.

During his early life Erickson developed polio and was confined to bed. Bored, Erickson started observing visitors closely noting their behaviour and body language. Erickson also watched his siblings from the time they crawled to when they were first able to walk. From these latter observations he taught himself to walk and was eventually able to leave his wheelchair.

Over many years Erickson developed a theory that each person has their own symbolic language or *psychological map of the world*. Successful treatment entailed helping the patient to discover and utilise their map.

Erickson talked to patients using their symbolic language (*metaphors*) in a similar way to which Freud and Jung were interested in patients' symbolic dreams. The crux of Erickson's method was establishing the meaning of the problem from the patient's point of view.

Erickson initially advocated auto-hypnosis whereby in a very relaxed state the patient could imagine themselves free of their problem and describe how life would be without it. From that point Erickson set patients tasks to enhance the healing effect.

Unfortunately later enthusiasts tried to rigidly mimic his methodology, including Erickson's physical hand and body movements. Erickson never intended this for he advocated therapists find their own unique method for treating patients.

## 2000 Anti Psychiatric Movement: Szaz & Laing

'In psychiatry we use one set of laws to explain sane behaviour which we attribute to reasons (choices) and another set of laws to

*explain insane behaviour which we attribute to causes (diseases).'*
*Thomas Szaz 2001.*

Psychiatrists Thomas Szaz and R D Laing held a controversial view that mental illness did not exist but was a construct of society. Laing believed psychoses held symbolic meaning. It is easier to explain by example so I will offer you a personal experience:

*Several months prior to a psychosis I had dreamt I was riding a motorbike when the fuel tank catch slipped open and the tank reared up in front of me. I calmly got off the bike and watched as the tank burst into flames.*

This dream has overtones of sexuality and impending danger. At the time of this dream my marriage was breaking up and I was virtually homeless and penniless. The dream indicated I would experience turmoil but recover (hence the calm feeling). The symbolism of a motorbike appropriately reflects my interest in machinery, archaeology and industry. If you are interested in dream analysis read C G Jung's *Man and His Symbols.*

The anti-psychiatric movement grew as *service users* (people who use mental health services), frustrated with the side effects of drugs and lack of effective treatments, sought other answers to their suffering.

The anti-psychiatry books by Szaz, Laing and their followers make interesting reading especially when seen in the light of 21st century patient preference for talking or complementary therapies rather than medication. However there are certain mind states which render the patient dangerous to himself or others and will always require drug therapy under our present day knowledge.

### Dialectical Behaviour Therapy (DBT)
Dialectical behaviour therapy (DBT) was developed out of CBT by American Psychologist Dr Marsha Lineham and was used for the

treatment of personality disorders and severe emotional problems. Patients who undergo DBT are likely to have felt criticised for most of their lives.

Dialectical means 'at either end'. The name reflects both ends of high emotional states experienced by people with personality disorders. DBT aims to pull the extremes together so the patient learns neither to hide nor overtly express feelings but make him or herself understood, to become less critical of others and at the same time less self-critical.

In DBT the relationship between therapist and patient has to be cooperative as they are dealing with a patient's core beliefs. DBT develops positive behaviour, promotes self-understanding and offers reward in the form of praise. DBT aims to build on individual success and spread change throughout the chain of unproductive behaviour.

DBT is a complex therapy, carried out by a team of therapists within both individual and group sessions and comprising 4 arms:
1. Learning to tolerate distress
2. Mindfulness – based on the Buddhist method for '*keeping in the moment*' as one goes about daily life
3. The regulation of emotions
4. Inter-personal effectiveness

## 21<sup>st</sup> Century - Ongoing Knowledge

### Virtual Brains - computer simulation

Real hope for rapid progress in the field of mental illness has come about through ongoing attempts to build maps of the brain using computer simulation (*virtual brains*). This will stimulate faster results for research into faulty genes responsible for serious illness like MDP or schizophrenia. Such research would normally take decades but computers vastly speed up this work. Perhaps we are nearing the time when mental illness becomes a thing of the past, like polio.

## DNA Research

Research into the biochemistry of the brain is bringing a sea change in the treatment of mental disorders. Scientists are using their increasing understanding of DNA to make headway into the causes and potential cures for mental illness. Drugs are more effective, side effects lessened and there is increased knowledge around the complexities involved when chemicals are combined.

## Psychopathic Personality Disorder and the Law

In early 2012, there was an interesting programme about the chemistry of psychopathic personality disorder (PPD). Although this disorder lies outside the subject matter of this book the discoveries have relevance to the increasing complexity of the relationship between mental illness, ethics and the law.

Two chemicals have been discovered as probable causes of PPD. This means that PPD in the future might become treatable but is certainly in the genes. What comes next runs into the realms of morality which worried early brain surgeons:

- how far should science interfere with personality?
- how would this be achieved on moral and social grounds?
- how would this affect the law?

In Tennessee, a man convicted of murder was found to have the psychopathic gene. The jury convicted him of manslaughter but not murder because he lacked the gene of conscience. However as the scientist involved tellingly explains, there is a great deal of difference between chemical factors and willfulness. He expressed concerns how this might be viewed by the courts and whether such people might literally get away with murder.

## Therapeutic Relationship

Therapeutic relationship has been recognized since the earliest days of the talking cures but is now scientifically recognized as a phenomenon with vital importance in healing.

During Professor Kathy Sykes Channel 4 programme CAT scans of patients showed how pain centres within nerve endings visibly reduced during spiritual healing sessions. Similar discoveries were made about acupuncture points.

## Neuro-Typical v Non Neuro-typical

The argument about what passes for normal is ongoing. With the discovery of conditions such as autism and high functioning autism (Asperger Syndrome) there has been more awareness of alternative realities.

Psychiatrists are used to putting clusters of symptoms into bands which describe illness such as schizophrenia but these categories have always been much debated because of the overlap. New thinking, borne out by research holds there is no such thing as neuro-typical; everyone has some kind of pathology.

With this comes a move toward the isolation and treatment of individual symptoms rather than an arbitrary attempt to divide mental disorders into clusters of symptoms with a label. A label is only a diagnostic tool but it is a much-needed explanation of something disturbing when it remains an unknown quantity. A label enables research, understanding, treatment and cure.

# Chapter 5

## The Mental Health Act 1983

**Content of this Chapter:**
Overview
Definitions of Staff within the Act:
Sections of the Mental Health Act

What follows is a very brief overview of the legislation underpinning the *sectioning* of patients. The professionals involved are described, an overview of the major sections and some rhetorical questions around the implications of the Act.

The Mental Health Act was brought into being to protect the public and those who might harm themselves during an episode of mental illness. Under its terms, people who were considered a danger to themselves or the public could be removed from society and sent for treatment in a Psychiatric Hospital (as the Asylums were renamed).

### Overview

The Mental Health Act 1983 was set up by the Government to regulate conditions for the '*reception, care and treatment of mentally disordered patients, the management of their property and other related matters*'. The legislation was designed to protect the public from potentially dangerous patients who might otherwise be discharged into the Community without supervision. As well as the legal part of the Act, a Code of Practice was drawn up for Health Authorities and Trusts upon which they could base their own patient care regime. The code contains:

1.  patient safety, privacy, dignity
2.  quality of care by hospital staff
3.  aftercare of discharged patients
4.  restrictions on detained patients who self-discharge

The Mental Health Commission was tasked with overseeing recommendations and making unannounced visits to Hospitals to check standards of care.

The Act was divided into Sections or chapters. Sectioning was often used as a slang verb describing how a person was taken into care i.e. *being sectioned.*

## Definitions of Staff within the Act:

The Act specified the responsibilities of each mental health professional when someone was to be sectioned. It defined the professionals and lay people who had a voice in the matter whether a relative or Court appointed official.

## Approved Social Worker

A qualified Social Worker trained to make applications under the Mental Health Act and to commit under a Section of the Act.

## Medical Referee

The Doctor (usually Psychiatrist) from the Hospital or it could be the patient's own General Practitioner. If a second reference was required this person had to be from a different Hospital and not a subordinate of the first Doctor. These measures were to:

*   prevent colleagues agreeing to a Section
*   prevent embarrassment if a junior disagreed with a senior

Medical referees could not be related to, or gain financially from, the patient.

## Mental Health Managers (MHM)

If the Hospital was run by a Trust the MHM was the Board.

## Mental Health Review Tribunal (MHRT)

Tribunal consisted of professional and *lay* members (members of the public). Tribunals were appointed by the Lord Chancellor.

## Nearest Relative

The *nearest relative* was a close relative of the patient; partner, spouse or parent. If a spouse they had to be living with the patient for at least 6 months and over 18 years. If no relative existed the Courts appointed someone to act in that capacity.

## Responsible Medical Officer (RMO)

The person responsible for the medical care was usually a GP.

## Sections of the Mental Health Act

*As you read the terms of the Sections try to imagine it happening to you or a close relative. Consider the vulnerabilities of patient and relatives.*

Applications allowing someone to be admitted to Psychiatric Hospital for treatment were made by an Approved Social Worker, Psychiatrist or GP who had seen the patient in the prior 14 days.

## Section 2 – Admission for Assessment

Two Doctors could detain a person for 28 days under Section 2. 28 days was a long time for anyone to be held in a Psychiatric Hospital for the first time.

*Could you cope with 28 days in the presence of un-medicated severely ill patients? Staff were used to strange behaviour and shouting but to someone newly ill this could be frightening.*

## Section 3 – Admission for Treatment

Section three was admission up to six months with extensions for six months then periods of a year. This is how some detainees spent huge tracts of time in hospital. Tribunals consisted of both professionals and lay people and were thus variable. This Section could be objected to by a patient's near relative.

*Imagine waiting for a Tribunal. If the Tribunal result was unfavourable your case might not be considered for a year. Imagine being a relative; would you have the confidence to oppose a decision made by a professional? Under what grounds would you feel this possible? Might you feel intimidated?*

## Section 4 – Emergency admission

This emergency Section required the agreement of a Medical Referee who could detain for 3 days.

*What if that Doctor was overtired, did not know the patient and had to make a hurried decision? What if the patient was of a different culture or particularly unconventional? Might this colour your perception? Remember these were life-changing decisions for the patient and their family.*

## Section 20 – Renewal (of a Section)

This section applied if a Doctor considered the patient might improve if they were held for 6 months or one-year periods thereafter. The renewal was aimed to protect the patient and the wider public from potential harm.

*Imagine someone detained for months or years. It was common for people to become institutionalized; so used to living in hospital they were unable to cope in the community. Asylums and hospitals protected people from cruelty but also affected return to normal life.*

## Section 23 – Discharge

Discharge was lengthy and involved a Tribunal. Relatives had a say but could be overruled by the Medical Referee or Tribunal.

*Consider how difficult it might be for a patient to prove they could cope. Might professionals be looking for illness rather than wellness? Would misinterpretations be possible? Might a patient afraid to face the community have a vested interest in remaining sectioned?*

## Sections 57 Consent to Treatment

This Section was consent to brain surgery [or hormonal implants in the case of a sex offender]. The patient had to give voluntary consent. Three Psychiatrists had to give a good case that treatment would cure or alleviate the condition.

*Consent by the patient depended upon how well the Doctor convinced them of the efficacy of treatment and an honest opinion on negative implications. But with little alternative, what else could they do?*

## Section 58 Consent to Treatment

Section 58 was consent for medication or ECT (Electro Convulsive Therapy) to be applied. Patients had to give informed consent which means they should be given information about the treatment involved and likely risks.

In cases where the patient was insufficiently mentally aware, the Mental Health Act Commission appointed a *Second Opinion Doctor* to act on behalf of the patient. He or she might give a go ahead even if the patient refused permission for this treatment.

## Section 93 - 113 Management of the Financial Affairs of Sectioned Patients

In some cases a *Court of Protection* would sit to appoint a professional with *Power of Attorney* over a patient. i.e. CoP gives legal permission for someone to manage the finances of someone with severe

71

mental illness. In all cases, the persons appointed had to keep financial records and report to the Court and were required to act '*in the best interests of the patient*'.

*Imagine you are mentally ill but there are lucid moments when you are aware of what is happening. During this time you realize someone is looking after your finances. Would that make you feel vulnerable? Would it be easy to let someone care for more of your life – i.e. opt out?*

## Section 134 – Withholding of Correspondence
This Section included:

- the right to open & withhold patients' outgoing mail [*if the addressee indicated they did not wish to receive mail from the patient*]ditto, if the MHAM felt mail would distress the addressee
- right* to withhold incoming mail in the interests of safety

*\* of the Mental Health Act Managers (MHAM)*

Accurate records had to be kept about withheld mail and its content. Mail addressed to MP's or legal advisers had to be delivered unless they gave written instruction such mail was unwanted. This maintained the right of the patient to write to their MP or solicitor. The patient could appeal to the Mental Health Act Commission for restoration of delivery except where the addressee had instructed otherwise.

*Manic patients might send letters with outrageous sexual content or highly personal remarks (in the throes of illness). In these circumstances what is your opinion regarding Royal Mail's duty to accept and deliver mail despite a recipient's objection? Would you want such mail? What if a deluded patient was seeking bomb making equipment, guns or knives?*

## Section 135 – Power to Enter (Private) premises

A Warrant had to be obtained by an Approved Social Worker (ASW) from a Justice of the Peace;

> Police could enter premises by force if necessary
> Police, Approved Social Worker & doctor to be present
> Patient was taken into a place of safety
> Patient could be held for up to 72 hours (3 days)

This Section dealt with persons in private premises believed to need urgent treatment. Sections were not issued lightly but medical opinions might vary about the severity of illness.

*Imagine you feel safe in your home although you are experiencing symptoms. You are taken from your home. You might not know what to expect. Would that increase your fear?*

*Imagine the distress of living with someone behaving in a bizarre way. Your relative might have attempted suicide or spent huge amounts of money under the influence of a manic illness.*

Families might wait a considerable time until an illness was considered serious enough to warrant Sectioning. The only other option would be for them to persuade their relative to go to hospital.

## Section 136 – Removal of People from Public Places

Police could remove someone from a public area for mental health assessment. The patient might be kept in a place of safety for up to 72 hours (3 days).

This was a controversial Section. Multi-cultural Communities had different social, spiritual and religious beliefs and there was room for misinterpretation of behaviour (remember the robed man). Police officers were not trained Mental Health workers although Health Authorities provided basic training.

*In extremist regimes many have been detained for political reasons under such Acts. How could abuse be prevented? Would you put public safety over individual freedom? How would you react if your relative was held? What would you do if your relative refused to go to hospital but was not ill enough to be sectioned?*

# Chapter 6
## From Detection to Diagnosis

***

**Content of this chapter:**
How Mental Illness is Detected
Mind (*function of the brain*)
Diagnosis
The Diagnostic Manual [DSM]
Undisclosed Cases of Mental Illness

### How Mental Illness is Detected
Who would recognise a problem had occurred

Two keynotes which denote presence of mental illness are differences in behaviour and mood. Changes might be so slight as to be tolerated until symptoms become marked. Changes might be marked (greater tiredness, increased energy; withdrawing from society or being outrageous); or they could be slight and therefore taken for normal mood or changes in energy levels. However, mood and/or behaviour can be attributed to normal events like bereavement, other loss or being given bad or good news.

The most obvious people to notice changes are family, friends or colleagues. Employers might notice decreased ability to carry out work. Or there might be emotional problems which were getting worse and had no apparent cause.

### How is a patient taken for treatment
Anyone can:
- go to their G.P. if they are worried
- be taken by friends or family to a Psychiatric Hospital
- be detained under a Mental Health Act

The patient might be treated by a G.P. or get a referral to a Community Mental Health Team and a case worker designated to make an initial diagnosis. Informally referred patients can be seen at home, in Surgery or a consulting room in a Psychiatric Hospital.

It is not always a Psychiatrist who diagnoses although [s]he is clinically responsible and will be the most qualified to prescribe psychiatric medication. A G.P. retains clinical responsibility throughout treatment. Mental Health workers meet weekly to discuss progress on patients, take new referrals and discharge patients. GPs receive reports on discharge or on demand.

## Physical and Mental Diagnoses

Diagnosis is the '*identification of disease by investigation of symptoms and history*'. Where physical illness exists a General Practitioner has many clues to help the diagnosis. If a patient has a painful leg and has recently fallen whilst skiing and the GP sees bruising and swelling, the G.P. might conclude 'You have a suspected fracture'. The patient, duly grateful and understanding his G.P's diagnosis would comply by having an x-ray in a local hospital. Following this he would accept the treatment of plaster cast, bed rest and physiotherapy. His relatives would be happy at the result and visit the hospital.

Matters are more difficult where the symptoms are mental rather than physical. The G.P. cannot look at his patient and make the initial statement 'You are mentally ill'. The G.P. would be likely to be taken to Court for defamation and the patient would not believe him. The patient might resist incarceration in a Psychiatric Hospital and resent being thought mad.

Even if patient and relatives accepted a mental problem exists the treatment (medication, psychiatric hospital, possibly ECT) would in all likelihood be rejected.

**Mind** (*function of the brain*)

The brain is a delicate instrument. It is controller of thoughts, feelings and actions. It controls the autonomous nervous system, (systems which function without thought; breathing, heartbeat, etc.). The brain has continuous use both waking and sleeping. Small wonder it occasionally malfunctions.

Mental illness majorly affects the mind. As we have seen, such illnesses can only be recognized through observing changes in mood, behaviour or reasoning (thinking) and in that way are more difficult to spot than physical disease or disorders. We considered these circumstances in the chapter about drawing the line between sanity and insanity.

No one knows where *mind* is situated although it is generally accepted to be an area inside the brain. Mind is the aspect of the brain where consciousness or awareness occurs. The part of the brain responsible for primitive survival mechanisms is in the brain stem, near to the base of the brain.

Although much is known about genetics and a lot about neurons [electrical messengers of the brain] little is known about mental processes and how they relate to outside stimulus.

It is accepted that mental illness is a complex product of internal and external factors such as thinking, experience, environment, genes, resilience – factors generally outside control.

When diagnoses are made they depend upon many factors; training, professional[s], culture, life experience, how the patient is feeling on the day, attitudes of the person diagnosing. Finally there is the vulnerability factor; how far the patient has support in overcoming symptoms, how chronic symptoms are, what treatment is available or how far symptoms can be alleviated.

Brain and mind are as unreliable as a car; they will not always safely take you to where you want to go.

## Diagnosis
Case History

The first action of a diagnostician (General Practitioner or Psychiatrist) will be to take a Case History. This is one of many strange terms used by the medical profession which means the professional sits with the patient in a Consulting Room and asks:

- the nature of the problems
- how the patient believes these problems occurred
- about the patient's physical and mental health
- if they have noticed changes in mood and behaviour
- how they are feeling now

They will then look at the medical history. All these questions will establish as far as possible:

- where the problems might have started
- how well the patient is able to deal with problems
- if there are pre-existing illnesses or diseases
- how long the illness has lasted
- how serious the problem is likely to be and the prognosis

Physical Examination

A professional might make other tests such as blood samples, psychological tests, physical examination. Mental illness can coexist with physical disorders and one can affect the other.

Medical Diagnosis

Finally the professional is ready to apply these factors and make a diagnosis i.e. an attempt to put a name to the illness. A name or label is not always positive but in medicine it enables a course of action to be taken.

## The Diagnostic Manual [DSM]

One of the tools a Psychiatrist uses to make diagnosis is a book called *Diagnostic and Statistics Manual* (DSM) the current being *DSM IV*. This American manual lists all the conditions (criteria) present in a particular illness. It is a kind of servicing manual – it lets the Professional know what they need to look for and gives a range of severity of symptoms.

The guidelines in DSM have been arrived at through research and observation of patients. Each condition has a set of numbers and letters allowing systematic diagnosis. Although this Manual is useful the professional also applies knowledge gained through clinical and life experience. Cultural and character factors are vital in making diagnoses.

DSM changes over time as trends change within social attitudes and with new scientific discoveries. For example plans are afoot to reassess the autistic spectrum replacing individual diagnoses with symptom clusters. Homosexuality once appeared as a diagnosis needing treatment whereas most enlightened societies accept this is as a normal type of sexuality. Bulimia and Anorexia have now been amalgamated under the general heading of eating disorders.

## Undisclosed Cases of Mental Illness

Mental illness can be treated only when people present to a GP or Psychiatrist. Millions of cases go unnoticed and untreated for a variety of reasons:

- family or friends might tolerate eccentric behaviour
- symptoms pass for normal in dysfunctional families
- mild to moderate depression can be seen as normal sadness
- mania can pass for exuberant or high spirits

- in certain cultures family is looked after at home
- where mental illness is shameful individuals are hidden
- mood or behaviour go unnoticed in isolated individuals
- symptoms might spontaneously disappear

There is no evidence that mental illness is purely a result of faulty genes. On the contrary it is accepted this vulnerability comes as much from exterior circumstances. What mental illness is NOT is weakness of character; I am happy to scotch that myth.

# Chapter 7

## Talking Cures

---

**Content of this Chapter:**
What is a Therapist?
How Do You Choose a Therapist?
Psycho Analysis
Psychotherapy
Psychology
Counselling
Mental Health Rehabilitation Worker
Social Worker

Although symptoms such as psychoses and delusions are treated with medication (which act at chemical level), psychiatric drugs are a relatively new innovation circa 1950 on. Prior to that, as you have read, mental illness was treated with talking cures.

In the 20th and 21st centuries, medication is used only for the most serious symptoms whilst talking therapies are commonly used. This is convenient when most people prefer to be treated in the community, disliking the stigma which remains around hospitalization or even outpatient clinics in psychiatric hospitals.

### What is a Therapist?
A Therapy according to my battered Oxford Illustrated is '*a curative medical treatment*'. A Therapist is therefore one who gives out curative treatment. One could argue it only applies to medically trained personnel but in this book I use the term to describe anyone paid professionally to treat patients / clients.

## How Do You Choose a Therapist?

If a patient is referred to a Community Mental Health Team a Therapist is chosen for that person. The Team meets weekly to discuss new cases and decide who is suitable and has space on their case list. Those who pay privately can choose.

## Length of training

Length of training varies but:

- younger therapists have less life experience
- the relationship between client and Therapist is vital

## Personal Experience – Vital for therapists?

Imagine taking a Ford to a mechanic. His theory is sound, he has repaired cars during his training. He will repair it adequately. Now imagine your car is a Porsche and your mechanic races cars and has re-built his own engine, in other words he is a specialist with personal experience. Considering the value of your car to whom would you entrust the repairs?

The brain is not unlike a finely tuned engine. There are ways in which it can cease to function properly which phenomenon we call mental illness. Mental illness has a plethora of diagnoses; schizophrenia, depression, phobia, anxiety to name but a few. However there are social symptoms and behavioural problems as well as physical symptoms. These make diagnoses complex.

## Psycho Analysis

Psychoanalysts (followers of Sigmund Freud) are a rare breed and not so well known. Their training is extensive and expensive as each Analyst has to undergo a training analysis lasting several years. To train a good Analyst is reckoned to take about 10 years.

Psycho = of the mind; analysis = investigation. Analysts investigate a sick (*neurotic*) mind by analysing faulty mental processes (*cognitions*).

An Analyst's job is to help patients become aware of the unconscious mental processes which are leading to difficulties. As these mental processes cannot be seen, an Analyst has to investigate from the patient's:

- **emotions** - emotions expressed when talking about difficult subjects e.g. are they angry when talking about parents
- **thoughts** - patients free associate and reveal unconscious factors which affect their mental stability
- **fantasies and dreams** – Freudians believe dreams to be the mind's way of revealing unacceptable facts or situations

## Psychotherapy

All schools of psychotherapy stem from the teachings of Freud and Jung but have developed into many different styles. It is impossible to generalise in a few lines but there are many primer books available on the subject.

Psychotherapies are talking cures. The patient/client speaks, writes, acts, or otherwise communicates his difficulties to the therapist. Some Psychotherapists use what is called an *Integrative method* based on more than one school of thought.

The job of the therapist is to help the patient understand why their problems occur. With benefit of this insight (understanding) the patient learns to recognise then change negative situations as they occur.

Psychotherapy patients attend to deal with a specific area of difficulty in their life whereas an Analysand (psycho analytic patient) might spend years in analysis to gain a broad perspective on their life.

Psychotherapy is not easy to undergo as it involved being open about situations which are difficult and often emotionally painful. It is not a quick option and can take months of intensive work. The length

83

of therapy depends upon the nature of the problem and the ability of the patient to absorb and put into practice what they have learned. Psychotherapy is generally not available on the NHS.

## Psychology

Psychology is the study of human behaviour and has its roots in Jung's work. Psychologists appear in different areas of life: education, employment, forensic (criminal) work, mental health.

Psychologists study animal behaviour and apply this knowledge to humans. They study behaviour, environment, family and conditions which might affect a patient's well being.

Cognitive behavioural therapy relies on the patient learning to recognize their own faulty thinking patterns and then change the behaviour that led to the problem. CBT puts faulty thinking and behaviour as the root of human discontent. Psychology is very structured in this way, more so than psychotherapy which uses a creative approach.

Clinical Psychologists work as Clinicians in hospitals. They take a three or four year Honours Degree in Psychology then specialist training to become a Registered Clinical Psychologist working with patients in Hospitals. Psychologists also work in research and publish professional papers on mental health issues. All Clinical Psychologists in the UK have to be registered.

## Counselling

The roots of Counselling lie in the village wise women. The seeker consulted a wise woman and received common sense advice based on the tribal culture and might also be given charms or herbs. Wise women were known to be highly skilled.

Although Counselling began as a complementary therapy Counsellors are now commonly found in NHS, University, G.P.

Surgeries and private hospitals. Counselling stemmed from the work of Breur, Jung and Freud.

Counselling can take many forms according to training and convention. This therapy is based on a therapeutic relationship between client and therapist rather than the autonomy of medicine with its prescriptive practices. Some forms are brief, based on the work of Milton Erickson (himself a follower of Breuer and Charcot). Others forms are of longer duration based on uncovering mental blocks based on the principles of Freud and Jung. There is also group therapy where a Counsellor conducts therapy among a group of clients.

Group therapy is a modern version of the ancient North American Indian custom of pow wows where the seeker squats in front of the whole tribe, who offer advice on his or her situation. The pow wow was also a legal court where misdemeanors would be punished, for example by a fine of cattle, excluding the individual from the tribe or a physical punishment. The Sharia Courts of Islam are an ancient example of community-based legal/social systems.

Counselling is an effective treatment for those with mild to moderate depression, emotional difficulties, bereavement, the result of natural disasters or practical concerns, the so called *worried well* with mental pain rather than active mental illness. It is not used in treating psychosis, depression of suicidal level or obsessional disorders which respond better to medication.

## Empathy

Those who have a great deal of life experience make the best talking therapists. Therapists who have problems and do not realize it or do nothing about it are not helping anyone, because they have blind spots.

The best choice of talking therapist is a matter of someone whom the patient respects. When considering therapists for the talking therapies you need to consider - has that person a deep understanding of the problem. How will you know this?

Empathy is not the same as sympathy. Empathy is an ability to understand someone's suffering without being emotionally crushed by that experience.

## Mental Health Rehabilitation Worker

Rehabilitation Workers (Rehabs.) used to receive on the job training on unqualified Social Workers scales but there is now a City and Guilds Qualification in mental rehabilitation. They are chosen for their maturity and breadth of life experience.

Rehabs in the UK work within a Mental Health Team and gather cases which do not readily fall into the other disciplines. Mostly, their caseload consists of patients with long-term mental illness who need Social Skills Training but they also take on short-term outpatients. A rehab's job might be considered as one of social education and social support.

## Social Worker

Social Work trainees have to be 22 years of age with some experience of working in the field or voluntary work. A degree in Social Work takes three years; the trainee gains a Degree (DipSW) in Social Work. Their training is in social policy, welfare and legal aspects of mental health with optional training in subjects such as addictions, psychology or learning disability. Social Worker trainees have to spend a proportion of their training on-the-job. Social Workers help patients with problems of day-to-day living. They might deal with housing, benefits, neighbour disputes, and general behavioural problems. Although there is a mild tag of social work being work done with working people they in fact work across the spectrum, also working with outpatients who do not have chronic mental health conditions.

Social Workers make legal applications for Sectioning under the Mental Health Act.

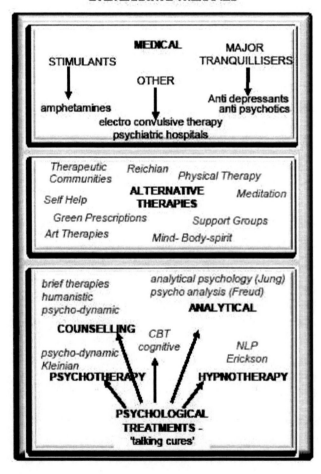

# Chapter 8

## Modern Medical Treatments

---

### Content of this Chapter:
Brain Chemistry Imbalance
Electro Convulsive Therapy (ECT)
Modern Drug Therapies
Stages of a Drug Trial
Categories of Drugs for Sale
Drug Groups
Antidepressants
Psychosurgery
Medical Practitioners

The hope of intervention by divine beings was once the only cure for mental illness with priests performing rites to exorcise the evil spirits believed to be the cause of bizarre behaviour and strange emotional states. This belief persists in some primitive cultures but medicine has largely taken over the restoration of balance and sanity.

The range of treatments on offer fall out of fashion as science pours new discoveries on mind and the genetic code. Medical treatments at present include (in order of preference):

1. psychological/ psychotherapy/ counselling
2. drug therapies (medications)
3. psychosurgery
4. electro convulsive therapy (ECT)

## Brain Chemistry Imbalance

Through long experiment it is now accepted that brain chemistry affects mood and behaviour. This is how human beings function as vital beings. Without behaviour change we would be like sheep with no opinion, will or ability to adapt to the changing environment.

### THE HUMAN BRAIN

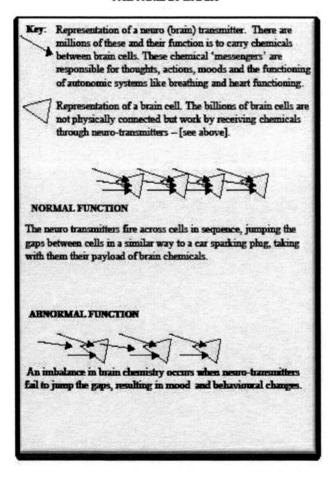

**Key:** Representation of a neuro (brain) transmitter. There are millions of these and their function is to carry chemicals between brain cells. These chemical 'messengers' are responsible for thoughts, actions, moods and the functioning of autonomic systems like breathing and heart functioning.

Representation of a brain cell. The billions of brain cells are not physically connected but work by receiving chemicals through neuro-transmitters – [see above].

**NORMAL FUNCTION**

The neuro transmitters fire across cells in sequence, jumping the gaps between cells in a similar way to a car sparking plug, taking with them their payload of brain chemicals.

**ABNORMAL FUNCTION**

An imbalance in brain chemistry occurs when neuro-transmitters fail to jump the gaps, resulting in mood and behavioural changes.

Mood and behaviour enable us to adapt to circumstances, appreciate nature and spiritual matters, turn envy into ambition and experience the better side of humanity and relationships.

Repetitive action teaches us to make new things, experiment, philosophise and overcome social circumstances. However, extreme imbalances in brain chemistry cause havoc. A sufferer can become so overwhelmed with mood and behaviour they become incapacitated, unstable or in extreme cases dangerous to themselves or others.

It is only extreme states that are generally referred to as mental illness although in this book I have included other mental conditions to broaden its scope. Mental illness encompasses personality disorders - but these are not in the remit of this book.

Although chemical imbalance theory is generally accepted, it is also accepted environment and family upbringing affect brain chemistry. The diagram illustrates the chicken and egg factor:

- is chemical imbalance purely internal?
- is it affected by external factors in the environment?
- is it a combination of one affecting the other?

Diet, drugs and alcohol are known to be contributory as are:

- birthing problems
- faulty genes
- accidental injury to the brain
- poverty, poor housing, severe life stress

There are no indications that social standing or education have a bearing on whether a person develops mental illness although extremes like poverty and bad environments definitely do have a negative effect. There is a cynical saying '*poor people are mad but rich people are only eccentric*. Mental illness knows no boundaries and affects kings, princesses and tramps alike.

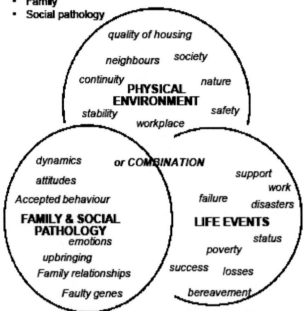

**BRAIN CHEMISTRY IMBALANCE**

*Brain chemistry is affected by:*
- Physical environment
- Life events
- Family
- Social pathology

quality of housing

neighbours    society

continuity    **PHYSICAL**    nature
              **ENVIRONMENT**
stability                    safety
        workplace

dynamics    *or COMBINATION*
attitudes                            support
                                        work
Accepted behaviour      failure    disasters
**FAMILY & SOCIAL**            **LIFE EVENTS**
**PATHOLOGY**                          status
        emotions            poverty
upbringing
Family relationships    success    losses
        Faulty genes        bereavement

*Brain chemistry, genetics (internal factors) AND environment, social relations & life events (external factors) all cause mood and behaviour changes which can result in mental illness. No one can isolate one causal factor for mental illness but most professionals would accept it to be a combination of all factors.*

Holistic practitioners believe mind and body are linked and the health of one affects the health of the other. Most therapists would accept this at the present time.

## Electro Convulsive Therapy (ECT)

A shock therapy using electric eels was favoured by Romans and was also used in Bethlem Hospital. After the discovery of electricity by Franklin (and later Edison) Psychiatrists experimented by pulsing low electric currents across the brains of ill patients. This type of ECT was used with some success for treating shell-shocked soldiers and depressive illness.

## Normal Functioning of Chemical Transmitters

Within the brain are millions of cells which are not physically linked but only through the action of chemical transmitters. The chemicals pass from one cell to another in a flow like electric current through a wire. An *electro-encephalograph machine* (EEG) readout shows the flow of current through the brain.

If the brain is functioning properly each cell receives a proportion of chemicals. Balanced brain chemistry results in a normal array of emotions and behaviour.

When chemical transmitters fail to work the result can vary from marked mood changes to bizarre behaviour and movements. When the chemistry settles through medication or other interventions most of these states are reversible (the equivalent of repairing wires in an electric cable). Electro convulsive therapy or ECT was used widely in the 1950's to attempt to deal with the problem of brain chemistry imbalance.

## Delivery of ECT

The first experiments with ECT were alarming. There are archive recordings showing a patient's body convulsing as nurses hold or strap the patient to the table to prevent injury.

In modern ECT a general anesthetic and muscle relaxant are given the patient to prevent physical injury and the currents are low. Electrodes (wires attached to pads) are placed on either side of the skull. The wires are connected to the ECT box which delivers an electric current. As the Psychiatrist switches on the current the shock causes convulsions in the patient's muscles rather like an epileptic fit. A course of around 12 was considered an average treatment when this therapy was initiated.

## Last Resort Treatment

During the 1950's to 1960's, ECT was used to relieve the symptoms of chronic depressive illness and schizophrenia. At this time there were few drugs available and the only other treatment for severe cases was incarceration in an Asylum.

No one knew how ECT worked only that it did in a small number of cases. Even at the time it was controversial because it lead to memory loss and personality change which might be permanent. The wards of the 1950's were filled with patients who had been damaged through excessive use of ECT.

Once drug therapy was introduced ECT was discontinued except for severe cases. Modern ECT delivers a current to one side of the brain at low voltage but even so it is rarely used.

## Modern Drug Therapies

What are Drugs?

Drugs are chemicals designed by Pharmaceutical companies to treat specific mental and physical illnesses. They work by intereacting at neuro transmitter level on brain chemistry.

New drugs have to be tested for years sometimes for over a decade. Only when they pass stringent tests can they be safely prescribed by medical professionals to patients.

The term *drug* is sometimes used as a slang term when describing illegal use of medication. Morphine, heroin, cocaine become illegal when purchased, used or supplied by persons not qualified to prescribe or be prescribed to.

Drugs can be curative and harmful. Sometimes even the medical profession makes errors and prescribes a wrong dose or a medication which reacts adversely with another drug (*contra-indication*). The drawback to drug therapy is that all drugs have side effects.

Psychiatric drugs replace depleted mood-changing chemicals in the brain. When delivered in the right quantities over a longish period of time the brain begins to function normally. As soon as the brain chemistry is restored drugs can be gradually withdrawn.

## Designing New Drugs

New types of drugs appear on the medical market all the time. Anyone on a particular brand for a long time will notice that from time to time their GP will prescribe a new one. The Pharmaceutical industry strive to improve the quality and effectiveness of their product, reducing side effects as scientists learn more about the human body and mind, and genetics.

Drug companies have to maintain a market lead in order to survive financially. There are huge costs involved in the design of new drugs many of which never come onto the market for reasons of safety or marketability. Drugs which prove interesting in the laboratory might fail human trials and have to be withdrawn. Refer to the diagrams which show the progress of a drug trial. Different procedures are laid for each drug trial.

## Stages of a Drug Trial

Preliminary– discovery and animal testing

Every Pharmaceutical Company has laboratories where scientists create new drug molecules. Molecules are the small particles from which all matter is made, from leaves to metal.

If a chemical looks promising for a new drug for a specific condition, scientists first develop the drug then conduct animal tests to see if benefits outweigh negative effects. Drug trials look for beneficial and negative effects on the diseases the drug is intended to alleviate.

Initial testing is carried out on laboratory rats, mice or dogs. A few companies test only on humans but such drugs contain proven chemicals already on the market. Scientists are looking for signs of *toxicity* (harmful) and *mutagenicity* (whether it alters or mutates the structure of the organism).

Careful documentation is kept at every stage as these are scrutinized by the drug licensing authorities who reject incorrect applications.

Phase 1 Testing – on volunteers

The next stage tests healthy humans, sometimes volunteers from the pharmaceutical company. They have to remain on the laboratory premises for the duration of the testing. Outside volunteers are paid well for taking part in trials.

Very toxic drugs such as those designed for treating cancer are tested only on patients (i.e. people who have the disease) not volunteers. Volunteer trials are aimed at discovering:

- how toxic the drug is, i.e. how well the body tolerates it
- how the body disposes of the drug
- comparative responses with people given blind trials *

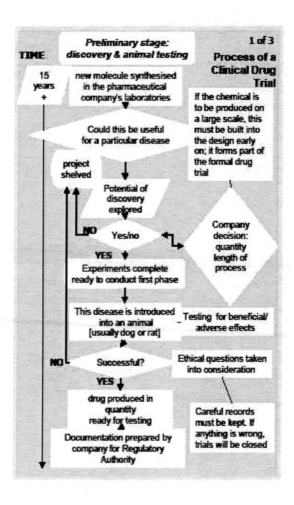

TIME

**Preliminary stage:**
**discovery & animal testing**

15 years +

new molecule synthesised in the pharmaceutical company's laboratories

Could this be useful for a particular disease

project shelved

Potential of discovery explored

NO

Yes/no

YES

Experiments complete ready to conduct first phase

This disease is introduced into an animal [usually dog or rat]

NO

Successful?

YES

drug produced in quantity ready for testing

Documentation prepared by company for Regulatory Authority

1 of 3

**Process of a**
**Clinical Drug**
**Trial**

If the chemical is to be produced on a large scale, this must be built into the design early on; it forms part of the formal drug trial

Company decision: quantity length of process

Testing for beneficial/ adverse effects

Ethical questions taken into consideration

Careful records must be kept. If anything is wrong, trials will be closed

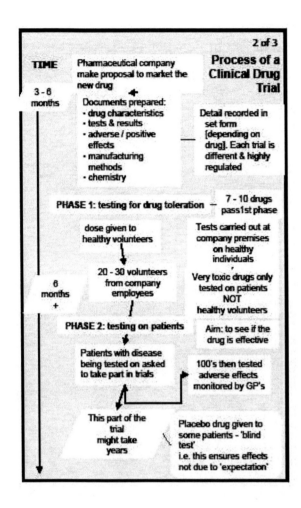

2 of 3

**Process of a Clinical Drug Trial**

TIME

3 - 6 months

Pharmaceutical company make proposal to market the new drug

Documents prepared:
- drug characteristics
- tests & results
- adverse / positive effects
- manufacturing methods
- chemistry

Detail recorded in set form [depending on drug]. Each trial is different & highly regulated

PHASE 1: testing for drug toleration — 7 - 10 drugs pass 1st phase

dose given to healthy volunteers

Tests carried out at company premises on healthy individuals

6 months +

20 - 30 volunteers from company employees

Very toxic drugs only tested on patients NOT healthy volunteers

PHASE 2: testing on patients

Aim: to see if the drug is effective

Patients with disease being tested on asked to take part in trials

100's then tested adverse effects monitored by GP's

This part of the trial might take years

Placebo drug given to some patients - 'blind test' i.e. this ensures effects not due to 'expectation'

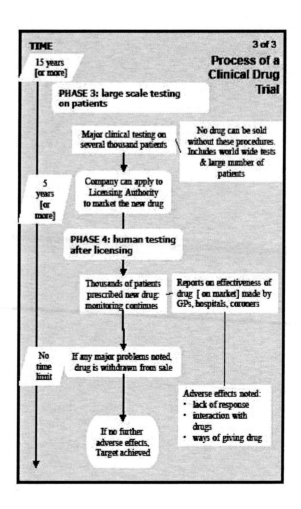

*blind or placebo tests where harmless substances are given certain volunteers to compare their response that of volunteers actually given the drug.*

A drug trial was halted a few years ago when volunteer patients developed extreme pain within minutes of the new drug being administered. The drug had been animal tested but something went wrong. Under such circumstances the trial is immediately halted and an investigation takes place.

Sometimes a drug is taken to a certain stage but a rival company gets to market first. When Viagra took the market by storm a rival laboratory quietly stopped trials for its own product.

### Phase 2 Testing – on patients

Once volunteer trials have concluded phase 2 tests commence on a small number of patients who have the relevant disease and have given consent to take part in a trial. If trials are successful, more patients take part. Applications are made for permission to make alternations to the procedure as trials progress.

Tests on patients show if drugs are effective, dosages at which they work and negative effects. Every drug has negative effects as currently it is impossible to *synthesise* (combine) chemicals and only have positive benefits. Perhaps when more is known about DNA structures in combination this will change. If a drug is found to have more side effects than positive ones it will never come onto the market.

### Phase 3 – large scale testing on human patients

This is a very important part of the drug trial procedure and determines whether the new drug is allowed a license without which it cannot be sold. A large number of G.P. patients are asked for consent to take part in the trials and are monitored for reactions to the drug. The purpose is to demonstrate if the new drug is more effective or less risky than drugs already on the market.

International trials may be conducted to gather a wide range of data. Once testing has been concluded satisfactorily a license is granted to market the drug commercially.

## Phase 4 – testing after the granting of a license

Even when a license has been granted testing is not complete. The Company conducts Phase 4 tests which show up difficulties in long-term use of the drug such as:

- adverse reactions in long-term use
- negative effects when other drugs are used at the same time (*contra indication*)
- revised dosage or administration of the drug
- looking at cases where it is not effective and establishing why

Once tests and large-scale trials are concluded all the negative effects are listed in MIMs (General Practitioners drugs manual) as side effects. All side effects have to be publicised by law even if they only occur in a few patients. Symptoms might be headache, nausea, stomach pains, vomiting or palpitations. When a GP prescribes he takes into account negative effects of the drug.

## Animal Testing

There has been much controversy about animal testing. In some cases drugs companies are able to conduct testing on tissue culture and thus avoid some animal research but these drugs still have to be human tested. It is questionable whether animal testing can be entirely avoided. Perhaps we had rather ask if we want to cure virulent and painful human disease and illness and thus continue to make animal testing a necessity in laboratories.

## Virtual trials

Following on from the above subject I came across a small piece whilst researching which mentioned new software used by Glaxo Wellcome (one of the largest UK based pharmaceutical companies).

The software can be manipulated to simulate behaviour of individual drug molecules. This helps cut certain early stages of the drug trial but whether it will have an impact on the more sophisticated testing on animal tissue I am unaware.

## Categories of Drugs for Sale

You may wonder why certain medicines are prescription only or cannot be dispensed unless a qualified chemist is present. The Medicines Act 1968 lays guidelines for four classes of medicines which can be sold over the counter in this country. There are:

- **GSL** or general sale list - over-the-counter
- **POM** or prescription only - only on G.P's prescription
- P or **Pharmacy** - only if the pharmacist is present
- **CDPOM** - dangerous drugs by GP hand written prescription

## Drug Groups

The diagram on the next page shows drugs that act upon the nervous system itself. There is a selection of plants used in holistic therapies which are reputed to alleviate symptoms.

Plants, roots, bark and berries were used as medicines thousands of years before pharmaceutical industries came into existence. Some drugs are still made from plant material. The following are examples of botanicals used as remedies:

- amaryllis belladonna (Belladonna Lily) –relief of Alzheimer's
- asarum canadense (wild ginger) – head colds
- curare –poisonous herb, muscle relaxant in surgery
- belladonna (deadly nightshade) –dilate pupils in eye surgery
- digitalis (foxglove) – used to regulate heart beats
- envallaria majatis (lily of the valley) – antispasmodic & diuretic
- mentha spicata (spearmint) –calming nervous disorders
- myrrhis odorata (sweet cicely) –anti cancer research trial

- salix purpurea (purple osier) –origin of aspirin
- tanacetum parthenium (feverfew) – migraine relief
- valeriana officinalis (valerian) – sedative

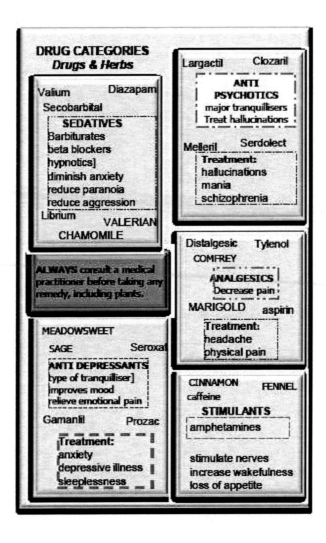

Wandering through the Botanic Gardens at Oxford I was struck by the beauty of these plants. Thousands of years use enabled herbalists to pass on plant therapies used to this day. This brings you in touch with man's lost relationship with nature.

Three groups of drugs which act on the nervous system are:

- sedatives – suppress the nervous system
- analgesics –act as pain killers
- stimulants – stimulate the nervous system

Sedatives are commonly used in psychiatry. There are two types, anti-depressants and anti-psychotics. Anti-depressants counteract depressive illness (mood control, relief of emotional pain, promoting sleep) whilst anti-psychotics reduce psychosis (hallucinations, delusions).

## Antidepressants

Antidepressants relieve symptoms of depressive illness but do not cure it. Depressive illness is complex and needs input such as psychological therapy and self-help. There are several kinds of anti-depressant medication which all work in different ways on the nervous system.

## Tricyclics

Examples of tricyclic anti depressants: Elavil, Endep.

Brain cells are connected only through chemical transmitters. This action maintains mood and behaviour. Two transmitters are serotonin and noradrenaline.

Tricyclic antidepressants increase the amount of chemical transmitter. This is like putting voltage across an electrical circuit; the appliance will do what it should whether it is heating water or powering a drill. In a brain, chemicals enhance or repress mood, reduce unwanted behaviour and assist sleep.

Tricyclic refers to the chemical structure of the drug which has a ring like structure. Even with medication it can take months to replenish natural brain chemicals.

SSRI's (Specific Serotonin Re-Uptake Inhibitors)
Examples of SSRI's: prozac, fluvoxamine, faverin.
Serotonin enhances mood.

MAOI's (monoamine oxidase inhibitors)
Example of an MAOI: marplan

Monamine chemicals control the fluctuation of mood. MAO inhibitors prevent a buildup of monamines and stabilise mood.

**Patient Compliance**

Patients can be prescribed drugs but unless detained under the Mental Health Act cannot be forced to take them. When patients say medication has not worked they may have broken off treatment early before the chemicals have become effective. This is common with patients taking medication for depressive illness who feel better and assume they no longer need medication but their symptoms return.

Another reason patients refuse medication is bad side effects. This ranges from parkinsonism, tics, stereotypical mouth hand or body movement, heaviness or numbness, reduced sensitivity or a general inability to think clearly.

For some patients medication is vital and without it they will not function. In worse case scenarios such as untreated schizophrenia or extreme personality disorders, patients can become dangerous to themselves or others. For others, not taking medication during depressive illness prolongs the misery.

## Psychosurgery

Brain operations are only carried out on very ill patients where there is no other option because they are very difficult and delicate to perform. Even in the 21$^{st}$ century we know relatively little about the functioning of the brain.

Modern psychosurgery is accurate and aided by a deeper knowledge of the physical brain, accurate scanning equipment and delicate instruments including tiny cameras.

## Medical Practitioners
### Psychiatrist

A Psychiatrist trains in General Medicine and obtains a Doctorate. After qualifying, they spend a year in General Practice before taking the extra training to enable them to become Junior Psychiatrists (around 6 months). It then takes up to 5 years to become a Consultant Psychiatrist. Psychiatrists are trained in all aspects of brain chemistry and the pharmaceutical drugs which are used to treat mental illness. They also train in either analytical or psychological therapies and the social knowledge and law which underpins this.

A Psychiatrist also administers ECT (electro convulsive therapy). Some go on to train in brain surgery or specialize in physical brain disorders such as mental handicap, Alzheimer's, brain injury or forensic (criminal) psychiatry.

Some senior Mental Nurses have additional training in psychiatric medication. Psychiatric medications are powerful and can be dangerous and are therefore prescribed only by medically qualified therapists.

### The Work of a General Practitioner

General Practitioners have taken a lengthy training of about seven years comprising examinations and on-the-job training in hospitals) and are deemed fit to practice general medicine. Competition for

Medical School is high and entrants have to achieve good science grades if they want to be accepted for MBBS Doctorate training.

General Practitioners study anatomy, physiology and biology as well as a specialist medical subject that takes their interest. Psychiatrists are qualified Doctors who have taken extra training in psychiatric medicine.

'Doctor' refers to the Degree or Doctorate in Medicine (MD). The term Doctor is used colloquially – i.e. 'I went to my Doctor the other day' but this is an incorrect use of the term.

## Registered Mental Nurse

Registered Mental Nurses take 3 year training, some in the classroom and some on-the-job at local Psychiatric Hospitals. They are taught to recognise symptoms of major mental illnesses and forms of therapy including behavioural therapies.

They also learn drug theory and at the end of this they are qualified to administer drugs. At present it is more usual for a GP or Psychiatrist to prescribe but advanced practitioners are now allowed to do so. Mental Nurses diagnose mental illness under Supervision from a Consultant Psychiatrist.

Mental Nurses work in a Community Mental Health Team [CMHT] usually attached to a local Psychiatric Hospital.

Incidentally, do you know how trainee nurses practice giving injections? They inject oranges, until deemed fit to practice on patients.

## Pharmacist

Pharmacists are scientists who specialise in the preparation and dispensing of medicines (drugs). Their profession dates back to the early Nineteenth Century when practitioners were variously known as

Apothecaries or Druggists or (more familiar) Chemists. Pharmacists work in Research Laboratories, Hospitals or Community Pharmacies. The last of these is either a specialist shop, part of a Chemist's Shop or maybe within a supermarket.

Students with excellent passes in science subjects such as chemistry and physics take the four-year Master of Pharmacy Honours Degree (plus one year post degree training. They learn:

- physical properties of chemicals
- chemistry of pharmaceuticals (drugs used as medicines)
- reaction of these chemicals in the human body
- how to measure correct doses

Pharmacists currently are not allowed to prescribe drugs and medication which is the province of the G.P. However, they can override a GP's prescription for drugs where the Pharmacist has reason to believe that the GP has prescribed wrongly or has proposed a drug which is incompatible with other medication the patient might be taking.

Pharmacists are allowed to recommend medications, provided these are licensed as over the counter drugs. Otherwise, their recommendations have to be prescribed by a qualified GP.

Confusing? It is at present, but this situation is currently under review* and it is highly likely that Pharmacists will in future be legally allowed to prescribe. Pharmacists are in fact more qualified in the chemical side of drugs than G.Ps by nature of specialist training.

*There is a Commission looking into changing this*

# Chapter 9
## Pen Portraits of the Therapists

---

### Content of this chapter:
Fictitious pen portrait and 'day in the life' to represent principals.

### Counsellor in Private Practice
Vera is a Counsellor in the school of Brief Therapy. She works in private practice as well as for General Practitioners. Her time is divided between counselling, teaching and training. She sees her Supervisor twice a week during which she discusses clients and receives feedback about her work. Vera pays for Supervision. A Supervisor provides an overview of Vera's patients as well as checking Vera's mental welfare is maintained.

Being in private practice Vera has to spend time finding clients, advertising (writing brochures and letters) and visiting GP surgeries as well as writing up her notes. Like any small business she produces accounts, chases outstanding fees and attends professional meetings. This means working more than a 37-hour week.

Brief therapists see clients for a fixed number of sessions, usually from 1 to 8 sessions. Each session lasts 45 minutes to an hour.

### A Day in the Life of Vera, Counsellor
Vera arrives at her rooms. Her client does not turn up but Vera waits in case he is late. 30 minutes later he arrives apologetically having forgotten the appointment. Vera has to be firm to not let him take the whole session or she will be late for her next. If she had a free appointment Vera would use her judgment about allowing more time because some patients are deliberately late for psychological reasons.

Tom is unhappily married and wants to talk about separation. He and his wife get on well as friends. Tom has a 9-year old daughter and is anxious about the effect of the relationship on her. The purpose of this early part of the session is to help Tom clarify his thoughts.

At the end of the Session Tom is clear he should separate but wants to consider how to provide for his family during this difficult time. He wants Vera to help him make a plan.

Vera's second client Jean is anxious about the disappearance of her daughter. In this Session Vera does not interrupt Jean's nonstop stream of words. Jean is less anxious when she leaves as she has a rare opportunity of airing feelings. Brief therapy uses more intervention than classic counselling but nevertheless the therapist needs to recognize when to remain silent. Sometimes it works like this, sometimes counselling is more two-way.

Vera's third client wants Vera to help with major decisions about a new career. At the moment she feels over involved with her children's problems and has no time for herself. This client is not distressed but needs guidance. Vera teaches this client problem solving to resolve her immediate crisis and as a useful tool for future issues.

After a break, during which she has to see a hostile Practice Manager about problems with noise outside the room, Vera sees two more clients before going back to her home/office.

She sighs as she sees the accounts and a pile of Case Notes– time for coffee and read the paper! She is about to make the coffee when the phone rings. It is one of the General Practitioners from the Surgery. He is worried about his patient and wants Vera to see the man quickly. Vera finds a free spot in her diary next day but it means she has to work late to catch up on her office work.

Her next call is from Tom's wife Megan. Tom told her that he was seeing Vera and Megan is angry. She wants to make an appointment with Vera to talk about her husband. Vera tells her this is unethical but offers to ask Tom if he will give permission for a joint session. Megan, still angry, is insistent and Vera has to spend time patiently explaining she cannot grant this request. Megan slams down the receiver. Vera sighs. This sort of situation is rare but she understands Megan's frustration. She is sure Tom will give permission but equally sure that Megan's hoped for reconciliation will not take place.

Relaxation is important for Therapists. Vera likes to relax by watching old movies, old Hammer horror films and science fiction. She hasn't counselled an alien yet but who knows? Vera will probably not spend all her career counselling as private practice is stressful.

\*\*\*\*\*\*\*\*\*\*\*

## General Practitioner

Dr Mason is a General Practitioner (G.P.') in his late 40's. He is the Senior Partner at his Surgery. He is qualified to diagnose, prescribe drugs, treat wounds and illnesses. He does not perform surgical operations nor does psychiatry unless he decides to undergo additional training. Some GP's undertake training in counselling techniques or psychiatry.

Dr Mason refers patients to other specialists and acts as a sort of clearing house between patient and Specialist. He takes *clinical responsibility* which means in law he is responsible for the physical well-being of his patient. Dr Mason is held accountable in law for his patient's life. Any specialist to whom Dr Mason refers a patient must report progress to him.

## A Day in the Life of Dr Mason, General Practitioner

Dr Mason has a morning Surgery at 8.30 am but arrives early to clear his administrative work. There are many statutory forms in the NHS and also a great deal of administrative patient work.

As each patient arrives the Receptionist finds their notes which are digitised. It is a legal requirement for all visits, medications and patient notes have to be recorded. Dr Mason is aware his patients have the right to see their notes so is careful not to write anything which could be misinterpreted. Some surgeries keep separate notes for details which might be detrimental if the patient saw them.

The Surgery is so busy Dr Mason has to limit each patient to 10 minutes during which he has to interview, diagnose and then prescribe. This is a short period of time so Dr Mason has to be adept at interviewing techniques. He leaves 2 appointments at the end of Surgery in case a patient needs an urgent appointment.

When his final patient leaves about 11.30am Dr Mason completes more paperwork, prints repeat prescriptions, signs forms and supervises colleagues. He might see representatives from Drug companies who will either want recruits for drug trials or to sell the latest medications.

When Dr Mason has agreed involvement in clinical trials for new drugs he has to keep detailed records for patients who have agreed to take part. Notes are kept on *effects* and *side effects* (unwanted physical or mental symptoms) of the new drug. This information is collated by drug companies and if the drug comes onto the market, it is written on both the packaged medication under 'warnings' and in the G.P. drug handbook MIMs.

Dr Mason oversees Junior Doctors working at the Surgery as part of their training. He employs a Practice Manager to look after the bulk of administration and may also employ a Manager to look after funding if he has his own budget. Once a week Dr Mason holds a practice meeting to discuss clinical matters.

Dr Mason covers emergency callouts twice a month work. Like Vera he attends meetings of a professional organization and training courses. Dr Mason suffers stress but unlike colleagues he attends a Counsellor when he realizes things are not right.

He finds it difficult to unwind after a busy day but enjoys Classical music concerts and the odd game of golf. Dr Mason is married but works long hours and his relationship is suffering. It is not easy to juggle his career with private life.

***********

## Registered Mental Nurse

Adrian trained as a Registered Mental Nurse during which he was taught medical theories about causes and onset of mental illness. He administers drugs as directed by his Senior Clinician (usually a Psychiatrist) and offers an opinion regarding type and dosage of the medication.  He gives depot injections to long-term mentally ill patients. These are injections into the buttocks or back of the hand given monthly. By giving a large dose monthly the patient suffers less needle pain than he would with daily injections.

Adrian also sees patients. He is trained in all aspects of mental illness and will carry out therapeutic work both in the Hospital and in the community. As a Nurse, Adrian also helps train junior Nurses a part of his work he enjoys.  He is studying for a Degree in Nursing and takes time during the day to write essays.

## A Day in the Life of Adrian, Mental Nurse

Adrian's patient Stan has long-term mental illness. Stan was diagnosed with schizophrenia 10 years ago.  Stan works full time as medication enables him to live a fairly normal life. Adrian is visiting Stan today to administer a depot injection.

Adrian sees Stan once a fortnight to support him socially.  Some patients have Social Workers, Occupational Therapists or Rehabilitation Officers as key workers but as Adrian sees Stan regularly for depots he feels it better to give Stan the reassurance and stability of visits by the same person.

It is Wednesday so Adrian attends the weekly team meeting. He has prepared reports on all his clients and reads these out. Adrian asks for advice on two cases. Anna (the Psychologist) wants to see Jessica and asks Adrian to set up a joint appointment. It is common for CMHT members to work together.

Adrian has a little room on his caseload so takes on two new clients referred from *Primary Care*. He asks Marlene to joint visit a second client who needs social skills training.

Adrian is attending his weekly session with his Supervisor. He likes to do this on the same day as the Team meeting as he makes Case Notes for both. During this Session his Senior Nurse notices Adrian is looking stressed and comments on it. He asks Adrian if he can cope with the extra two on his list. Adrian is relieved and agrees he is taking too much on. The Senior works with Adrian to rearrange his diary.

After lunch Adrian calls Mrs Abrahams who is suffering panic attacks. She has recently been bereaved of her teenage daughter and she and her husband are finding it hard to come to terms with the loss. Adrian offers to arrange an appointment with CRUSE a charity specializing in bereavement counselling.

Adrian does not feel well and decides to take the advice of his Senior to cancel his last appointment and have an early night. Tomorrow will be another day.

**********

## Occupational Therapist [OT]
Petra trained for 3 years during which she learned among other subjects theories for the cause of mental ill-health and about the different kinds of disability. She is able to advise patients on disability

allowances, suitable equipment for their living quarters and suitable work and activity.

Petra spends much of her time in patient's homes dealing with patients who are suffering physical as well as mental health problems. She enjoys working in the Community rather than having a similar role within the Hospital: her friend Jackie works in such a role with severely disturbed patients.

## A Day in the Life of Petra, OT

On today's first visit, she is helping Gina overcome agoraphobia. Petra has been working on a graduated programme which will enable Gina to visit her sister who lives a mile away. Today, they have managed to get Gina 100 yards from her front door. This may not seem a large achievement but remember that it has taken Gina 10 years to get this far.

After leaving Gina, Petra drives to the team room to complete case notes and call Social Security about an application another client has made for benefits. She talks to colleagues over lunch then drives to her appointment with Vanya.

Vanya was crippled in a car crash two years ago. Vanya is trying to come to terms with the emotional and physical realities of life in a wheel chair. She is on the case list of the Mental Health Team as the stress triggered depressive illness.

Vanya has asked Petra to look at the equipment in her kitchen and living room. She is finding it difficult to maneuver her wheelchair around the kitchen and grasp items for food she is preparing. In the living room she needs grab rails to help her move from her wheelchair into her chair.

Petra is feeling tired. She still has to collect her son from Nursery School and make another call to see Arthur. Sometimes Petra realizes she is spending longer on calls than she has the energy to cope with. Her Supervisor has discussed this with her and asked Petra to do something about it

.

\*\*\*\*\*\*\*\*\*\*

## Community Based Pharmacist

John Jethro prepares some of his patient's pills himself. He is a qualified chemist and enjoys this part of his work as many medications are off-the-counter commercial preparations from pharmaceutical companies. John is happiest, when his customers ask for his advice as it makes his work more interesting. Not many of his customers realize he is a highly trained scientist and knows more about drug chemistry than General Practitioners.

By law he has to be in the shop when medicines are dispensed in case his customers need to ask questions about how the medication has to be taken:

• with or without food
• number of times a day
• if foodstuffs 'contra-indicate'\* with the medicines

*\*some foods react with medicines making it ineffective and other foods are dangerous when taken with certain medicines.*

## A Day in the Life of John Jethro Community Pharmacist

9.00am Friday and the Shop is about to open but John is late. Sally, one of the assistants, serves a customer with toiletries but the lady then wants a specific medication. Sally knows she is not allowed to sell this unless the Pharmacist is on the premises. Her customer is annoyed as she is in a hurry but Sally has to be firm. Luckily, John arrives and he is able to dispense.

The shop is busy and John retires into the pharmacy to mix tablets for one of his regular customers. As it is Autumn, he decides to get in more stocks of influenza and cold medicines. He knows through experience which brands are most likely to sell.

After lunch a representative from a pharmaceutical firm arrives with samples and John goes into the back office with him. Just as the Representative is leaving the telephone rings. The local Hospital have a cancer patient who needs a certain drug, and their supplies are exhausted. The Pharmacist they use at another Hospital has been called away on an emergency and there is no one locally who has the necessary qualifications to dispense. John dispenses the necessary supplies and hands it to the motorcycle courier who has been commissioned to transport the drugs to the Hospital. All drugs have to be carefully accounted for, so that if any get into the wrong hands there is a trace system.

All is well and John adds an extra quantity of the drug to the order which Sally is about to place. Sally has prepared a list of out of date medicines which have to be destroyed. Sally and John make an order to two larger suppliers which Sally faxes across.

6.00 pm and the shop is officially closed but John and Sally are still busy. John sees the local drug addicts at this time to pick up *scrip's* (prescriptions). Addicts are prescribed legal chemical substitutes such as methadone which lessen the worst effects (cramps, hallucinations) when they attempt to give up hard drugs after years of use. Many Pharmacists set aside time outside normal shop hours for this task. They know customers can become upset at the wild appearance or behaviour of some addicts and have to protect their business interests.

6.30pm and at last they put on the alarms and lock up. Another busy day's trading. John is looking forward to a half-day's lecture he is giving over the weekend to trainee Pharmacists at the local University. He is looking forward to the day when Pharmacists can prescribe drugs and he can gain public recognition for his pharmaceutical training.

**********

## Psychiatrist

Psychiatrists such as Mr Lacey treat mental illnesses with drugs designed to alter brain chemistry. His patients are offered appointments from ½ hour to one hour, which is considerably longer than the 10 minutes slots allotted to General Practitioners patients.

Paul Lacey deals with what are called *forensic* cases. He might deal with paedophiles as well as patients with psychopathic personality disorder. Publicly these people might be reviled but Paul has to view them as patients who need treatment otherwise he would not be doing his work properly. If Paul Lacey and his colleagues believe a patient to be untreatable then there would be no hope for that person because above all Psychiatrists must remain non- judgmental.

## A Day in the Life of Paul Lacey, Psychiatrist

8.30 am and Paul is already looking at his list of patients. The list is full and there are appointments in the Psychiatric Hospital as well as community visits.

First visit is to Gannoway Prison where he is to see Mac. Mac is an habitual alcoholic in his 60's who is not expected to live. Mac suffers from schizophrenia. He stabbed and severely wounded his brother Joe, under a delusion that Joe was an alien in human disguise. Mac is in prison because there is nowhere else suitable. A secure hospital 20 miles away has no beds and there are none at the smaller unit in the local Psychiatric Hospital.

Paul has a soft spot for Mac who is a likeable character when his delusions pass. Mac is a good cartoonist and is drawing when Paul enters his cell, a portrait of a devil and an angel arm-wrestling, in grey and blue chalks. Paul persuades Mac to take a depot injection and eventually Mac agrees.

Mac likes being in prison because he feels secure and is well fed. He has no home and knows the *screws* (Prison Officers) and regards them as family. Mac feels lonely as his family refused to visit since the incident with Joe and hopes he will not be given parole at his next prison review. Sadly he is likely to commit another offence if released in order to stay in prison. There is little other choice and he feels more secure in an institution.

Next call is at the Hospital where Paul is running a Seminar for Junior Doctors. He enjoys training others. One of his Trainees is convinced a new therapy has cured a long-term patient. Paul knows the patient in question has been experiencing such 'cures' for 20 years but he does not like to dampen the enthusiasm of the trainee. He suggests his student observes the patient longer before making conclusions.

An anxious Mental Nurse hurries toward him in the corridor and asks him to see the patient in the next room. The patient has severe depression and is sitting in the room not responding. Paul asks questions about the patient before making an unscheduled visit.

Pamela is sitting on the floor her head in her hands. She is distraught. By gentle questioning Paul ascertains her partner has left, unable to cope with her illness. Now she has financial and housing worries on top of her original problems. Paul offers reassurance and arranges for a Social Worker to call to her home.

The Nurse is grateful but is embarrassed he had not thought of this practical solution. Outside the therapy room Paul suggests that the obvious is not always apparent when we are in a panic, a lesson the Nurse is learning.

Paul is late for his next appointment with a lady suffering mania. This is a very distressing illness not only for the patient but also her family. This lady, Marcia, is accompanied by her daughter Ann. Ann is very distressed. During the height of a manic episode Marcia had taken £8,000 out of her bank account and given it to a very dubious charity.

Marcia is extolling the virtues of the charity while her daughter is crying. Ann tells Paul her mother is behind with her mortgage payments and likely to lose the family home. This kind of situation is not unusual amongst such patients who are not aware of what they are doing under the influence of this illness. Unscrupulous people take advantage of such situations.

Paul is unable to stop Marcia talking and sees she is getting deeper into her manic episode. He cannot legally section her under the Mental Health Act, as her actions are not a danger to her life despite the ruinous financial implications. However, he does persuade Marcia to have an injection of Haloperidol which will reduce her manic level.

After helping Ann get Marcia safely to bed and talking to Ann about Adrian providing some social support Paul leaves. He is angry as he dislikes patients being abused yet knows in this situation there is nothing legally he can do to intervene.

Late afternoon finds him in his office writing case notes and lecture notes for student doctors. Each week he likes to attend the Journal Club which gives advanced training to Junior Doctors. It is one of the few occasions they can meet up with peers during the working day.

On his days off Paul likes to swim and play golf. He finds it hard to fit in the work he loves with the responsibilities of a large family (4 children all under 9 years). He has to be careful his marriage does not suffer under the strain of long working hours which are unfortunately a normal part of his routine.

**\*\*\*\*\*\*\*\*\*\***

## Psycho Analyst

Analysis is generally not available on the NHS because of the cost and time involved. Patients are expected to attend from 2 to 4 sessions a week each session lasting 45 minutes. The former is often referred to as the *therapeutic hour* as the last 15 minutes is used by the Analyst to complete patient notes.

Peter has been a Psychoanalyst for 10 years. His training lasted 5 years much of that spent working with a senior colleague with regular sessions to discuss clients. Before that he had to undergo a training analysis lasting several years.

## A Day in the Life of Peter, Psycho Analyst

Peter takes his dog for a walk first thing each morning to refresh his mind before starting work. Analysts concentrate hard on what their patients bring and this takes a great deal of mental energy although Analysts enjoy their work and find patients stimulating as well.

Peter has only three clients today. He is due to see his first, Stella, at 9.30am. She sees him twice a week for 45 minutes. Stella has been his patient for 3 years and is about to conclude therapy. She referred herself after a very unhappy childhood followed by an unhappy15 year marriage. During the marriage Stella lost confidence and wanted to work with Peter to find a better future for herself. She also wanted to work out why the marriage had failed so if she re-married things would be different.

During these 3 years Peter mainly listened allowing Stella to work things out for herself. He occasionally would repeat back (*interpret*) what she said in order help her become aware of her unconscious thinking.

Stella experienced many dreams during her analysis which she described to Peter. Through these dreams, which were sometimes violent, they uncovered Stella's anger towards her father (now deceased) which she had been unconsciously directing toward her husband.

Peter takes 15 minutes after Stella leaves to write up her notes. Analysts do not make notes during their time with their patient relying on their memory. They believe note taking in a session is intrusive and they might miss vital information if distracted in this way.

121

His next patient is Jester who chose that name himself but is in fact a sad man gradually recovering from a schizophrenic illness. Not many Medics believe this illness can be treated with analysis. But Peter seems to be having remarkable success with Jester, an intelligent man who has been in analysis for 5 years.

Peter has been helping Jester over a series of *delusions* which centre around a bizarre circus and its performers. Peter had an *intuition* that this circus represents feelings and emotions Jester has been bottling up. After working for many months Jester's delusions are reducing and he is beginning to deal with difficulties in real time.

As Jester leaves Peter sees his third client of the day driving up the lane. This is a new patient, Marilyn. She is early. Peter signals out of the window he has seen her and then completes his notes on Jester before going down to let her in.

Marilyn is cross at being kept waiting and expresses this by deliberately knocking one of his plants off the stand as she enters the room then watching for his reaction. He smiles inwardly. Is this how she expresses anger in everyday life? The process of analysis begins.

Peter loves classical music and lovingly draws his violin from its case. A little Mozart today, perhaps? He lives a full life. He has learned from experience how important that is.

***********

## Clinical Psychologist

Psychologists like Anna treat patients with behavioural therapy or cognitive behavioural therapy. Whilst accepting the chemical theory of mental illness they are not medically trained and do not prescribe drugs.

Psychologists conduct research on the work they do and publish clinical papers on the basis of evidence gathered from their interaction with patients. They also conduct research in the community for example upon the social effects of mental illness in families.

In order to become a Clinical psychologist Anna will have studied for a Degree in Psychology followed by further training of 3 or 4 years. She will then become a junior Psychologist and train on the job, working on wards before she can register.

Anna like many other trainees had been interested in human psychology from an early age. She had a difficult childhood and an innate curiosity about why people behaved the way they did. It was this curiosity which drove her towards training in psychology.

Eventually she came to realize that though psychology held interesting answers about life it was by no means a cure for every problem. That aside she enjoyed her time with fellow students and kept in touch by attending professional meetings and events organized by the British Psychological Society.

## A Day in the Life of Anna, Clinical Psychologist

Jenny (one of Anna's patients) has experienced great cruelty by her father in childhood and now becomes very frightened at work when her male bosses criticise her, often bursting into tears then becoming embarrassed. Jenny keeps making mistakes at work and is beginning to lose confidence. She is also becoming depressed.

Jenny is not aware that her childhood experience has a bearing on her current fear of men. Anna would term Jenny's behaviour towards men as a *negative behaviour pattern*. Jenny herself calls it '*the silly way I am*' and although she is aware of what she is doing she can't seem to stop herself.

Anna uses cognitive behavioural methods, which will help Jenny become aware of how her childhood relationship with her father is being repeated in her adult working life. By bringing this *behaviour*

123

*pattern* to her patient's awareness Jenny can to work towards more productive behaviour in the future.

Anna visits the ward to see her long-term patients most of whom are diagnosed with schizophrenia. There is as yet no cure for this illness but advances are being made with medication which helps control their delusions and hallucinations.

Anna sees her role as trying improving the life of these patients by bringing order into their chaotic world. She devises social rehabilitation programmes which are carried out by the Occupational Therapist or a Rehabilitation Worker. Simple tasks such as washing, dressing or cooking are difficult for someone with schizophrenia because they lack concentration and can become overwhelmed with delusions. A structured day is not only socially beneficial but also comforting to the patient.

After seeing patients and talking to ward staff about the management of the programmes, Anna returns to her office to write up case notes. This is an important part of the work and takes a considerable amount of time. Notes are required so that other professionals can refer to them when Anna is not there.

In the afternoon she is on a community visit to a patient with a severe depressive illness. Sandie should be in hospital but her husband is adamant he wants her at home where he can keep an eye on her. This makes Anna's job difficult but as the lady has not yet shown serious suicidal intent she agrees.

Anna spends time listening and sitting with Sandie who is quiet and subdued. Sandie's husband Jack keeps running his hands through his hair. Anna feels it important for him to be present although like many men he finds it hard to cope with his wife's sadness.

Anna has explained to them why depressive illnesses occur and how they are treated but feels this information needs to be repeated. People under considerable stress do not take in much information.

After 1½ hours, which is a long time in therapeutic terms, Anna leaves the house and drives to her next appointment for a training session at a Community Health Team. She has agreed to train local staff in Behavioural Therapy techniques as their Psychologist is abroad. Training is part of her role and enables her to refresh her own memory at the same time.

After training she talks to the Team Manager before heading off to another Community visit where she meets up with Eric. They are visiting a man strongly suspected of sexual abusing his two grandchildren. This will be a difficult visit emotionally as well as professionally.

The man is abusive and aggressive in contrast to his wife who is weeping and distressed. The man admits the abuse but is unable to see he had done anything wrong. 'She asked for it' he says adamantly; the 'she' in question is 7 years old.

Eric finally has to call the police when the man starts to attack his wife in front of them. There is no cure for personality disorder but mental health services have to offer treatment and protect the public. The man will be visited in his police cell by Dr Lacey and will use evidence from this visit in the legal case.

By now it is the end of the working day. Anna has one more patient, a lady almost cured of agoraphobia (fear of open spaces). Anna has been working with Patricia for several months until Patricia has walked to the Hospital unaided. It is difficult to imagine what an effort this has been but Patricia shows her delight by giving Anna a present, a beautiful crystal paperweight. Staff normally are not allowed to keep gifts but as this is for Anna's desk she accepts.

Anna spends an hour with Patricia. They have already agreed this will be the final session and it is emotional. Professionals are trained not to become emotionally attached to patients but they are human beings and bound to have feelings. Anna decides to go home after this to relax.

***********

## Psychotherapist in Private Practice

Alison sees clients for an hour once a week and probably a longish term of about a year or longer. Alison will explore with her client the day-to-day difficulties and try to understand exactly what is happening and why.

Alison lets her clients decide on the issue to be talked about. However, if she feels her client is evading something or trying to deal with too many areas at one time she will bring this to their attention so they can re-focus the session.

Alison was a teacher before deciding in her 40's she needed a change of direction. After spending months deciding she finally went to the library and looked up the entry requirements for re-training as a Psychotherapist. Many people decide quite late in life to train in one of the Therapies and this is looked on favourably as older therapists bring a wealth of life experience.

Alison does not wave a magic wand and make people better. She is a person who had problems in her own life, resolved them, then decided she liked people enough to devote her career to healing others. Alison likes to be with her family in her free time. She loves her home and prefers time there to holidays.

## The Case notes of Alison, Psychotherapist

Our Psychotherapist Alison is seeing David today. David has difficulties in socialising though he is an intelligent and attractive man. David finds it difficult to express his feelings when he meets a girl he likes and after a few dates breaks off any budding relationships. Then he becomes depressed and angry.

One week David starts to tell Alison about a time his favourite pet dog was run over but was unable to cry although he wanted to. He and Alison spent the hour talking about other occasions when sad things happened and David found himself unable to express emotion.

Towards the end of the hour David suddenly remembered that as a child he had cried when his favourite teddy had been thrown away in the rubbish accidentally. For David, that teddy bear had represented a friend. His father had beaten him with a strap and told him not to be such a baby.

Remembering this in the session with Alison David began to cry copiously. In fact he cried for ½ hour unchecked. Alison gently asked him why he was crying and David said it was the first time he could remember not being punished for crying. They were then able to talk about feelings and how wrong his father was not to have let David express his too human emotions.

Alison would have been very pleased David cried. This would be what she called an insight; in other words he was learning to understand why he bottled up feelings.

A good Psychotherapist like Alison would only see 4 or 5 patients in a day as this type of work is emotionally demanding. Supervision and writing case notes take up a good deal of time as does the ongoing training necessary for all therapists.

***********

## Rehabilitation Worker

Marlene has a flexible job. She had no formal entry training as in her time Rehabs were chosen for their common sense and life experience. They received on-the-job training whereas now there is a City & Guilds Certificate in Rehabilitation. Marlene has to deal with the more difficult of the Team's cases, chronically mentally ill patients. She uses a good deal of judgment, both to determine what her patient needs and how to achieve that end in a friendly, relevant and acceptable way.

Marlene is no servant to her patient and team. She will have to persevere when most have given up, to accept her patient's bad behaviour on occasion. All this for the lowest salary in the team.

## A Day in the Life of Marlene, Rehabilitation Worker

Marlene has a patient called Yvonne who has long-term depressive illness. Marlene visits Yvonne weekly to take her shopping. Marlene has devised a long-term programme designed to build Yvonne's confidence.

Marlene suspects that Yvonne is developing agoraphobia and wants to prevent this for it will only add to the problems. She has arranged to visit Yvonne at 11.00am and uses the two hours before this first visit to catch up on housing applications she has made on behalf of two of Eric's patients. She rings the Housing Office and discovers several questions need further information. Luckily she has time to visit the Housing Officer and complete the forms.

Today Yvonne is feeling better but is anxious about the state of her home which became untidy during a recent *episode* of depression. Marlene helps her to clear up. This is not part of her job but she considers it practical rehabilitation for her client who will benefit psychologically from the better environment.

Afterwards they devise a written agreement for Yvonne to do small amounts of clearing every day and also to deal with the post she would otherwise let pile up. Depressive illness takes a large amount of physical energy and what would normally be simple tasks can become overwhelming. The plan will give a focus to Yvonne's day during difficult times. Therapists often ask their patients to formalize such a plan by signing it like a contract.

Marlene's second client is Rob who has been bereaved. He needs to talk and be reassured. Marlene arranged for him to see a CRUSE Bereavement Counsellor who will visit him at home twice a week. Rob cries a good deal during Marlene's visit and talks in detail about Jen's death.

Marlene is training in Counselling but she cannot deal with Rob herself as she has recently been bereaved. Mental health workers have to be aware of their own mental condition and not see patients when they cannot cope with their own emotions.

Marlene visits Sal, a teenager who lives in a bedsit two miles from her parents home. Sal's parents are tolerant and supportive but concerned because she visits them three times a day and is far too dependent on them. She also wakes them very early in the morning by banging on the door. Sal is a pleasant girl whose delusions are fantastical rather than frightening (she sees and hears Angels) but at heart she is lonely and has poor self-care.

Today Marlene is helping Sal compile a shopping list and plan what she is going to eat for the week. An O.T. in training had made a food plan but it proved too complex for Sal who only had a limited attention span. Marlene decided to simplify it. Sal liked to eat convenience foods so they planned readymade pizza, prepared salads, baked beans and fruit. Marlene knew Sal would not be able to cope with shopping and cooking of complex meals and would go back to her old habit of crisps and chips.

Marlene's next appointment was with Richard, a senior Executive at an Electronic Company, who had become stressed through over work. Richard was wary of being referred to the Community Mental Health Team and thought they only saw mad people. When the G.P. explained he could be visited at home he agreed.

Marlene introduced herself and explained the role of the team in Community Mental Health. Marlene explained to Richard how stress was an integral part of living but that excessive stress could build and affect physical health, even bringing on heart attacks.

She went on to explain stress in detail and showed him how his symptoms (inability to remember, tendency to lose vital documents and sometimes hearing voices) were normal in these circumstances. Richard was relieved as he was afraid he was going mad; this is a common misperception.

By now it was 5.30pm. She wrote up her case notes and was about to leave when Esther rang.

Esther was a patient with a diagnosis of mania. Marlene was fond of Esther but in small doses! Esther frequently rang the office when she was high and needed someone to talk to. Esther lived with her aged mother who was deaf. Marlene arranged to see her after the Team Meeting. She knew Esther had not taken her medication and left a note asking Adrian to visit and check up on this. Finally, about 6.00pm, Marlene left for the day, just in time to attend her evening class in Photography.

***********

## Social Worker

Eric our Social Worker took a Diploma in Social Work several years ago and is now a seasoned member of the Mental Health Team and a guardian of the public who come into his domain.

Many people on Eric's casebook will be permanent patients with chronic, enduring mental illnesses (schizophrenia, MDP, OCD). Others might be outpatients with short-term difficulties.

There is still a stigma attached to having a Social Worker as some folk have an old-fashioned view that only working class people need them.

## A Day in the Life of Eric, Social Worker

Eric's first appointment is to visit Susie who is about to divorce and needs social support and financial advice. A court case is pending about the sale of her marital home. Susie is living with her small daughter in Council bed and breakfast emergency housing which Eric helped her find.

Today he is helping her with Housing Benefit forms and to look at possible part time work. Susie is stressed as this situation is unfamiliar and she is really worried about the future for herself and her daughter. Just before he leaves Eric teaches Susie some relaxation techniques and leaves a music tape which he made for her the night before.

Eric has a couple of free hours so he returns to his base. A welcome cup of coffee with colleagues is followed by a visit to Sam, one of his longer-term patients.

Eric needs to give Sam a depot injection of drugs which stay in Sam's blood system for about a month, ensuring he stays sane. They talk about Sam's progress while Eric monitors Sam's mental state. Sam's conversation reveals how strong or weak his delusions are. They also share news about a joint love of model aeroplanes.

Every week after the injection Sam goes to a day centre. When the bus arrives, Eric visits his next patient Monica. He parks near a field to eat his packed lunch as his call book is full and he has no time to return to base.

Monica is not answering her door and Eric is concerned. He knows she is in as he saw her rushing upstairs as he rang the bell. Eric knows Monica has not been well for weeks. She has a diagnosis of schizophrenia although she refused depot injections.

Eric suspects she has not been taking medication and needs to be in hospital for assessment. Her neighbour recognises Eric. She tells Eric that Monica has been running around her flat late at night shouting.

She is concerned Monica is looking frail and thin. Monica has broken an upstairs window.

Eric decides he needs to apply for Sectioning under the Mental Halth Act and calls Dr Lacey on his mobile. He drives back to base and a few hours later has the papers ready. He returns to the flat with a Police Officer who has a warrant for forced entry.

After the Police Officer has broken in Eric finds Monica shivering in her bedroom. She has soiled and wet her clothing and the flat is in a filthy state. Eric takes a frightened Monica to Hospital in his car and the neighbour arranges to have the flat boarded up. Nearly an hour later Monica is in a hospital bed and has been given injections to help her sleep.

Eric is too late for his next appointment and telephones to re-make. Juggling is necessary as each day brings different needs. His last appointment at 6.30pm is help Matt complete benefit forms. Eric is thankful this will be straightforward. He and Matt complete the forms and eat a plate of biscuits. Eric's partner Sally is aware his working hours are erratic and is tolerant of his lateness on some evenings. He arrives home at 7.30pm

.

**********

## Hypno-Psychotherapist

Jason was a banker who in his spare time devoted himself to Community work. He had taken training with CRUSE bereavement counselling) and RELATE (relationship counselling) after doing voluntary work but realised he wanted to become a professional in private practice.

After months agonising and talking to his family he decided to undertake Hypno-Psychotherapist training with a School which offered training over weekends. Weekend training is becoming common for adults who have to earn a living during the week.

Jason found it tiring, working as well as training and research but felt the future benefits outweighed the not inconsiderable time spent on his new career. He discovered early on he was expected to deal with his own life problems first. This was not easy as like many men he found it hard to discuss feelings.

## Case History -Hypno-Psychotherapist

Nearly 18 months later and Jason has started his own private practice and has several patients. His supervisor is Mandy who has had her own practice for decades. He sees her once a week for about 2 hours depending on how many clients he is seeing.

First through the door is Andy who has facial twitches. These are uncommon and very distressing. People can be cruel and Andy has been teased about winking on numerous occasions, not only by children but also adults.

Jason takes a case history and asks Andy about the nature of the twitches (sometimes referred to as 'tics'). When Andy relates the large number of tics and also the fact he gets very angry easily Jason starts to consider Andy might need a different kind of treatment. He suspects Andy does not have a simple tic but a form of Tourettes disorder which needs medical intervention.

Andy is naturally upset. He thought a few sessions of hypnosis would be enough. He is afraid of Psychiatrists (like many others). However, Jason persuades him that medication might be effective and help with mood problems as well. He offers to refer him via a colleague he met at his training school and finally Andy agrees.

His next client is Daisy who is about to go on holiday but is afraid of flying. She booked the holiday hoping it would give her an incentive to overcome her illness as her family long for a holiday abroad. Jason will have to work fast as the holiday is three weeks away.

He takes a case history and discovers that the phobia (fear) occurred after a traumatic flight when turbulence caused her flight to crash land on the runway. Unfortunately on her next flight a man tried to hijack the plane albeit unsuccessfully. Since then Daisy had been afraid of aeroplanes.

Jason spent some time reassuring Daisy these incidents, although in a short time frame, were highly unusual and unlikely to reoccur. Jason relaxed Daisy into a hypnotic state (trance or very deep relaxation). First she was to imagine the events as they were. Whilst doing this Jason noted her breathing rate rapidly increasing and her fists clenching. In the second trance she had to imagine the same events but this time with a different outcome, i.e. alter her breathing and concentrate on this rather than events around her. This took Daisy a while to get used to but by the end of the hour-long session she was feeling better. Jason decided to see her twice more encouraging her to practice concentrating on breathing and hand movements.

Daisy was able to get on the aeroplane albeit nervously. There was turbulence but she put herself into a trance state and coped. Several years later Daisy is still happily boarding planes with her family. Hypnotherapy and Hypno-psychotherapy are useful for dealing with specific problems of short-term duration. Trance states are also used by other therapists as an adjunct when client relaxation is an issue.

**********

# Chapter 10

## Institutional Care & Support Groups

---

**Content of this chapter:**
1990's Care in the Community
Psychiatric Hospitals
Self Help - Support Groups
Therapeutic Communities

Local newspaper report
*'[An] arsonist... who has served 21 years in jail, is on the move today. The man who put him behind bars, Judge... wrote 'In a just Society ... he should not be in prison at all, but in a secure place, where he could be offered and receive treatment.'*

### 1990's Care in the Community

*Loneliness. I saw a man from a local Group Home, a house in the community where he had been moved from his long-term home in a now closed Asylum. He was standing on a street corner singing to himself, cradling a pile of incontinence pads held close like a baby in his arms. His face expressed incredible sadness.*

Many patients did not want to leave their Asylum homes where despite crumbling, draughty buildings they had supportive staff and generally a welcoming community. The villagers had long become used to bizarre behaviour and generally tolerated it.

Although the community was tolerant about patients when they returned dutifully to their Asylum at night it was different when the Government decided all must live in the community.

Patients went to live in communal or group homes, houses purchased privately in residential areas. Three or four ex in-patients lived together under one roof, compatibility being a matter of judgment, luck or medication. Some patients were offered Council bedsits and left to their own devices most of the week. Each home received support visits from mental health staff, one or two visits a week or more for severely ill patients.

Some patients moved into isolated bed-sits could not cope. There was a spate of petty crime by individuals, many with enduring schizophrenia, desperately hoping to be sent to prison in which institution they felt safe. Prisons became congested with seriously mentally ill people.

Care in the Community was based on the premise that the Community cares. The reactions of the public ranged through tolerance, indifference and hostility. There was an instance where a so-called sane person threatened to shoot patients about to be housed next door to him. The authorities bowed to this threat and the patients were housed elsewhere.

Former Asylums were pulled down or converted to luxury flats. Where patients had lived their lives in wards with peeling-paint and ancient heating systems, these became the luxury dwellings of their former detractors. Many Asylums were obliterated from history, with not even a street name to acknowledge the past.

There is a montage of images of former asylum St John's Hospital, Stone near Aylesbury. All my photographs of Stone are now in the Buckinghamshire local history collection.

## Psychiatric Hospitals

The last of the old Asylum buildings were now being decommissioned in favour of new but smaller psychiatric Hospitals.

With the advent of better medication it was no longer necessary to lock up vast numbers of human flotsam for decades.

The Care in the Community Act gave responsibility for day care to the Psychiatric Hospitals with a few beds for respite care for those incapable of living independently. Criminally insane patients were imprisoned in psychiatric prisons such as Broadmoor and Carstairs.

An average 1990's Psychiatric Hospital might consist of one or two permanent wards, an outpatient department for day cases and teaching facilities for junior Psychiatric staff. Rooms would be available for therapists (Psychiatrists, Mental Nurses, Psychotherapists and Mental Health Workers) to see out patients.

There were specialised services such as art therapy, group therapy and public classes for the so-called worried well on subjects such as assertion and stress management. Community mental health charities might use meeting rooms for specialist therapy - Alcoholics Anonymous, Cruse and Relate Counsellor training, or for self help groups run by mental health charities such as Mind or Rethink.

## Self Help - Support Groups

There are many support groups, variable in type and content, run by a plethora of individual mental health charities. The fact that patients attend these to share experiences does not mean they will like or get on with the other folk in the group or else find the format agreeable. However, support groups fill a gap between NHS services and the private sector. Many people find them invaluable especially on long, lonely Bank Holiday weekends.

There are virtual support groups for those with access to the Internet and computers are now provided at all main libraries. There are millions of virtual support groups across the world. The Americans may be faulted for many things but looking after themselves is not one of them.

Support does not mean attending a physical group. Books and magazines are also supportive. There is nothing like shared human experience to lessen isolation even for those who dislike one-on-one human company.

## Samaritans

Founded in 1953 by Chad Varah, an Anglican vicar who wanted to find a way of alleviating the suffering of the suicidal, this voluntary organisation has 200 branches nation-wide and over 20,000 volunteers. Samaritans went online in 1994 offering confidential email to users in addition to telephone lines.

Volunteers from all walks of life undergo a selection process followed by training of about 30 hours and six months probation. These volunteers are selected for their life experience and are supervised and supported. These folk provide free all-year 24 hour listening to fellow human beings who have reached the lowest levels of despair and need an objective listening ear.

## Therapeutic Communities

An uncommon form of treatment, Therapeutic Communities consist of therapists and seriously ill mental health patients living in a communal building. The Community is self-functioning and self governing, existing to deal with such long term difficulties as addiction, behavioural problems, personality and emotional disorders.

Patients are encouraged to take part in the management of the Community and hold weekly meetings to discuss difficulties and socialize as well as group therapy sessions in which everyone is expected to join.

Each day is highly structured and consists of therapeutic activities interspersed with chores such as gardening, cleaning, and DIY projects. Therapies can range widely and include some of the those not offered mainstream, for example:

- art therapy
- psychodrama
- gardening therapy

Also offered are standards likes group therapy, women's and men's groups and group psychotherapy.

There are drawbacks to this idyllic situation. Therapeutic Communities can be a potential hot pot for exchanging illnesses as well as giving a potential for real growth. However, for those who experience difficulties in community living, these are undoubtedly among the best option combining understanding with therapy.

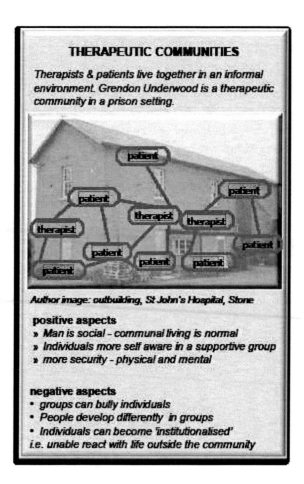

**THERAPEUTIC COMMUNITIES**

*Therapists & patients live together in an informal environment. Grendon Underwood is a therapeutic community in a prison setting.*

patient

patient

patient

therapist

therapist

therapist

patient

patient

patient

patient

*Author image: outbuilding, St John's Hospital, Stone*

**positive aspects**
» *Man is social - communal living is normal*
» *Individuals more self aware in a supportive group*
» *more security - physical and mental*

**negative aspects**
• *groups can bully individuals*
• *People develop differently in groups*
• *Individuals can become 'institutionalised'*
*i.e. unable react with life outside the community*

# Chapter 11

## Case Histories:

**Contents of this chapter:**

Brief Psychotic Disorder - Jane
Depressive Illness - Sally
Eating Disorder - Fiona
Mania - Emma
Obsessive Compulsive Disorder (OCD) - Cynthia
Personality Disorder - Tom
Phobia - Mike
Schizophrenia - Mandy

The following are simplified case histories designed to characterise symptoms of a range of mental illnesses. I have set out recognized symptoms from DSMIV together with causes and treatments or remedies.

In order to make this more interesting, have a go at symptom spotting. **A Note** - *please do not take this exercise too seriously. Mental illness it is not for lay diagnosis. If you are worried about yourself or someone else, visit your GP.*

Please remember to prevent unnecessary worry that I have described extreme cases to highlight the symptoms. In real life no patient has every symptom nor are all outcomes portrayed here. There are also cases in which treatment is either rarely successful or simply not available. It would be dishonest of me as an author if I did not present this information. Even in the 21$^{st}$ century we know little of how the brain and mind operate.

## Brief Psychotic Disorder

Brief Psychotic Disorder is a medical term for what is commonly known as nervous breakdown. The name describes the condition well; an illness of short duration during which the patient loses touch with reality (*psychosis*).

Psychosis is a symptom of many serious mental health disorders. Brief psychosis is of short duration, a fragmenting of the mental processes as a result of overactive chemicals in the brain. *Psychosis* means out of touch with reality. What the person sees, hears and feels during a psychosis is real to them but not to others around them.

If confronted with a psychotic person, they will not be seeing you; you will have become the object of their delusion. Those who commit murder under delusion are not deliberately choosing to kill an innocent. It is as if they are an actor in a virtual reality film.

Patients are unable to carry out normal living being engrossed in an imaginary world where sensations are heightened and frightening. Sleep is fitful. Delusions and hallucinations resemble ongoing nightmares such that the sufferer is unable to distinguish night from day. Classical art features '*day into night*' as a theme.

The film *A Beautiful Mind* vividly depicts the hallucinations and delusions suffered by Dr John Nash who was diagnosed whilst at University with schizophrenia.

## SYMPTOMS:

Physical

- Speech unclear
- Withdrawal from every day activity
- Dishevelled appearance
- Agitated.

Mental
- Delusions –has fixed ideas or beliefs at odds with reality
- Hallucinations –sees or hears things that are not there
- Inability to concentrate
- Extreme fear
- Confusion about time orientation [*day into night*]

Causes
- major life stress
- following childbirth
- extreme stress states
- after trauma and battle injury
- after bereavement

## Attitudes

People are generally sympathetic to those who develop brief psychotic disorder. They recognize this is not the patient's fault and that the disorder can be treated with hospitalization and medication. As it is common after birth, women tend to talk about it rather than perceive it as shameful or frightening - stigmas common among the general public.

## Cures/ Remedies
- medication to reduce psychotic symptoms
- detainment in Psychiatric Hospital
- supportive counselling

## Case History - Jane

'If I knew I had to go through this again I would kill myself. It was like being in hell. I thought 'they' were following me trying to control my mind. Everyone was in the plot even my Doctor and my husband. I could trust no one. I went to bed afraid and woke up sweating and frightened. It was a nightmare - only the nightmare went on day and night. If I had not gone into hospital when I did I might never have recovered.'

Jane is 40 and separated after years of marriage. Neither the marriage nor Jane's childhood were happy. She has no family and lives a solitary life except for her clerical job in an insurance company.

Jane has a small number of friends. She is not a life and soul of the party type but her friends appreciate her quiet manner and ability to make them feel cared for in difficult times.

Her friend Joe noticed Jane's answer phone had been left on for two weeks. Although it was customary with Jane not to answer every call such a length of time was unusual. When he called at her flat the curtains were closed and he noticed an upstairs light on though it was still light. Joe rang Cynthia, a mutual friend. Cynthia said Jane had not attended a writing group which was unusual as this was Jane's favourite outing.

Next morning, Joe and Cynthia called Jane's employer who said she had been acting strangely over the past few weeks. She had been losing things, getting angry and her work was not up to standard.

Joe and Cynthia called the Police. A warrant was obtained to enter Jane's house. A Police Officer and Social Worker met Joe and Cynthia. After some delay Jane answered the door. Her friends were shocked by her appearance. Jane looked terrified and refused to allow the Police in.

The house was in a mess with litter and half-eaten meals in every room. Cynthia tried to hug Jane but she backed off, crouching in her chair, rocking and shouting at someone she could obviously see but no one else in the room could.

The Social Worker asked Jane a lot of questions. Jane said she had been to her GP a few days previously but had to rush out as a man in the waiting room was listening to everything and making notes. All this seemed real to Jane.

The Social Worker took Joe and Cynthia aside and said he would have to detain Jane under the Mental Health Act and take her to a Psychiatric Hospital. Joe asked if he and Cynthia could take her. He was aware that, were Jane to be committed (*sectioned*) she might have difficulties with her employers who were not sympathetic. The Social Worker agreed.

After a couple of hours of coaxing Jane was persuaded to go to Hospital. She was admitted that evening and Cynthia was allowed to stay with her in the ward until the medication sent Jane to sleep.

Next day when the Consultant Psychiatrist arrived Jane began to show fear. A Mental Nurse gave Jane a tablet but she refused to take it. Cynthia asked the Nurse to leave,, then asked Jane why she was not taking the medication. Jane said the Psychiatrist was trying to poison her.

Jane's belief was so strong that Cynthia could not persuade her otherwise. The Nurse injected Jane with a drug which put her to sleep. Cynthia and Joe continued to visit over the next few weeks and noticed an improvement. The delusions started to disappear and she was looking in better shape.

Jane was terrified by her ordeal and found it difficult to talk to the Counsellor the GP recommended. However, eventually Jane revealed personal details which Joe and Cynthia did not know about. In one session, Joe and Cynthia were present with Jane's permission, talking about how they might support Jane.

Several weeks after entering Hospital Jane was discharged and continued her counselling from home. By now she was embarrassed and smiled at the thought the Consultant had been trying to poison her. A year or so later Jane found the confidence to find a more demanding job and to build a new life. The symptoms did not return.

**********

### Depressive Illness

Untreated severe depressive illness can be lethal. People of all ages and all different walks of life take their own lives under the delusion their relatives will be better off without them.

Depressive illness has many causal factors, both internal and external, which are described in the symptoms section. It is an illness and not ordinary life sadness. There is a depth of suffering which is not always apparent to the onlooker, even family, which is why many people feel guilty for not spotting it in a relative or friend.

When depression is chronic it cannot be treated with talking cures. Medication is required to rebalance the brain chemicals [serotonin and nor-adrenaline]. This can take a considerable number of months or years, but a degree of relief can be obtained within a relatively short time after receiving medication. Depressive illness is common.1 in 4 people will be treated for depressive illness at some time during their life.

Telling a depressed person *pull yourself together* is as helpful as giving the same advice to someone with a broken leg. However, people worry too much about what to do when a relative is seriously depressed. Human contact and comfort is all.

The most destructive and misunderstood symptom of chronic depressive illness is suicide or suicidal urges. These are not under the control of the sufferer as they will not be thinking rationally; it is a form of delusion. For example, suicide notes reveal people saying irrational things like '*you will be better off without me*'. Sadly, some suicides take their children with them, again under the powerful delusion that they will be better off 'with God' for example. All this is highly distressing for those left behind, who have to deal with the resulting anger, guilt, trauma and shock.

## SYMPTOMS
At least 5 of the following symptoms must be present almost every day:

Physical
- Sleep disturbances (lack or increase of)
- Lack of energy
- Decrease or increase in physical movements
- Changes to weight and appetite (increase or decrease)
- Withdrawal from activity and social life

Mental
- Persistent low mood (*marked irritability in children & teens.*)
- Tearfulness
- Lack of concentration or decisiveness
- Lack of pleasure in everyday life and activity
- Feelings of guilt or worthlessness
- Thoughts or desire of death

Causes:
- Changes to brain chemistry
- Family history of the illness
- Abuse of alcohol or drugs
- Loss e.g. bereavement, amputation, job, opportunity, relationship, some precious object
- Life events of all kinds

Cures/ Remedies
- Medication to supplement brain chemistry
- Electro Convulsive Therapy (ECT)
- Cognitive-Behavioural Therapy (*when recovering*)
- Counselling (*when recovering*)
- Mindfulness or meditation training (*when recovering*)

## Sadness and Depression

The adjective *depressed* is wrongly used to describe sadness. The difference between sadness and depression is the difference between a cold and pneumonia. Depressive illness is an imbalance in brain chemistry which blocks chemicals responsible for well being.

Clinicians use testing systems of which the most well known is the Beck Depression Inventory (BDI). This is a questionnaire with multiple choice answers each of which has a score. The scores are measured against a scale which indicates severity of illness at the time the form is completed. It only works when the patient is honest answering the questions. Beck's tests the shifting pattern of depression.

People fear being considered weak (particularly males) and try to keep depressive illness hidden often becoming angry or irritable instead. People are afraid of suicidal impulses. Some people seem to believe the illness can be spread like a virus. Certainly it is distressing to be around someone who has been depressed a long time although contact with friends and family benefits patients.

## Suicidal Urges

Suicidal urges can be very strong but the patient's inability to do anything about the urge can prevent suicide in the depths of the illness. Suicide more often occurs when recovery starts and patients have enough strength to carry out a plan. It is vital that anyone expressing suicidal impulses is taken for assessment and cries for help are not ignored. People are not being dramatic, they are strongly expressing need.

## How Long Does it Last?

Depression is not easily treated and requires support from family and friends as well as medication. Even with medication, it can take months until the brain chemistry rebalances or life events trigger permanent change, but during this time there will be periods of relief.

## Case History – Sally

'It was like being at the bottom of a pit. No ladder was long enough to pull me out. All the time I felt a shadow following me – my Black Shadow. But even when I remember sitting in a chair at home unable to move I was aware of friends visiting and later that comforted me. I could not respond at the time and sometimes I didn't even want them there. But all the time I was really saying for God's sake don't leave me alone. It was the most isolating experience I have ever had. Every day I thought how sweet it would be not to have to wake up.'

Sally had reached her 46th birthday. She was very unhappy having suffered periods of depression all through her thirties which had never been treated although several times she had half-heartedly seen a Counsellor.

Sally never liked to talk about feelings and would break off therapy to avoid feeling uncomfortable. Sally suffered so long she had almost become used to her illness which she called her Black Shadow. She was one of many people so familiar with their illness they give it a name as if it were a tangible object.

Her mother had a history of depressive illness and died age 46 after a very unhappy married life. Her aunt had committed suicide. Sally thought often about her mother. She regarded her mother's life as being wasted on the wrong person and was angry at both parents for an unhappy childhood.

Sally married John, a kind man but one who also found it difficult to talk. When she became depressed he would anxiously do things for her and found it difficult to understand what was happening to his wife.

Over several months Sally had become more withdrawn. If John tried to talk to her she snapped or burst into tears. She would sit around for long periods doing nothing as the house became dirtier and the washing piled up. Sally no longer had the energy or inclination to make love and rejected John's advances.

John felt rejected and stopped trying. He started an affair. He tried to avoid Sally by going to the pub sometimes coming home drunk. Her friends could not cope with her suffering. When they visited Sally she sat in her chair not responding.

Whereas most people would feel alert after a night's sleep, Sally woke feeling heavy and tired as if she had had no sleep. Most of the night she had lain awake thinking repeated thoughts about the worthlessness of her life. In the mornings it took Sally hours to get dressed. Getting out of bed was an effort. The bed was a secure place for her. Though the bad feelings were still there it gave a bit of sanctuary from what she experienced as a hostile world.

Eventually Sally stopped bothering to get up. Feeling more and more isolated despite the efforts of her partner Sally decided it would be better to die and started writing a note. Luckily John came in and saw what she had written and was shocked. He took the bull by the horns and insisted Sally immediately went with him to their GP.

Sally's G.P. prescribed ante-depressant medication to lift her mood and made an appointment for her to see a Psychiatrist. John was reluctant for his wife to go to a Psychiatric Hospital because he thought only *mad* people went there. However the G.P. reassured him these places were for anyone with mental health problems. After a short hospitalisation Sally could attend as a day patient.

John asked how long Sally would have to take antidepressants. The G.P. said it might be several months, once week to start with and then lower doses as she recovered. Sally could see a Counsellor to help her regain confidence. The G.P. wanted John to be involved in Sally's treatment with her agreement.

Throughout this period Sally's recovery was erratic. However, she was reassured by staff. At the same time, John found a Counsellor to deal with his own problems. He was given information about relationships and depression and felt less guilty as he realized Sally's depression was not his fault.

As Sally recovered she and John realized they were no longer in love and hadn't been for some time. Although it was a sad decision they knew divorcing was best for both of them. Sally wished her own mother had taken the decision to divorce as her parents made the childhood home very unhappy with arguments.

Sally started training for a new job as a Nursery Nurse. She decided to stay in the house she and John had lived in to give herself security. John visited and they were able to talk freely for the first time in years. Sally started to make new friends although she preferred being in her home for a long time before she finally ventured out.

During the next few years Sally relapsed but each time she felt stronger and able to seek help when she needed it. In time the symptoms disappeared.

***********

## Eating Disorder

Formerly divided into *anorexia nervosa* and *bulimia nervosa* eating disorders are now grouped under one diagnosis which is still notoriously difficult to treat. Anorexic types tend to restrict intake of food whereas bulimics tend to binge eat then purge (using laxatives or through vomiting).

It is not that such patients do not want to eat; they often crave food and are obsessed by it. The drive to not eat and purge are impossible to control. It is frightening for the patient as well as relatives. As well as these urges there is strong malfunctioning of self-perception. People find it hard to understand how teenagers weighing 6 stones or less think they are fat. It is an illness of perception (*body dysmorphia*).

Eating disorders affect 1% of the population with a growing tendency among teenage boys.

Do you remember being a teenager and thinking you were fat and when you were older re-visiting your photographs and being surprised you were a normal size? It's the same mental trick being played in the minds of those with eating disorders. Such negative perceptions are difficult to shift. Force-feeding ensures survival but to cure the illness requires the patient to see themselves as of a normal weight.

Patients are cunning about concealing and destroying food even whilst hospitalised. There comes a stage when the body organs cannot cope with the lack of nourishment. Unfortunately a high proportion (25%) of seriously ill patients will die from organ failure.

## SYMPTOMS
About 2 episodes a week over 3 months of the following:

Physical
- Body weight fluctuation
- Recurrent vomiting or purging (by patient) or restricting food
- Teeth decayed because of stomach acids from vomiting
- Menstrual cycles disrupted and may disappear altogether

Mental
- Fear of gaining weight (anorexia)
- obsessive about body shape & weight

Theoretical Causes
- History of family problems
- Fear of growing up and facing independence
- Bullying or teasing at school especially about appearance
- Desire to control themselves or their families
- Media obsession with body image

## Attitudes

Even among medical staff this illness is misunderstood and nurses have not been kind. Families are devastated. Imagine seeing your child deliberately self-starving but you can do nothing. With knowledge and a deeper understanding of psychological approaches the outlook is improving.

## Cures/ Remedies

- Compulsory hospitalisation with a strict feeding regime
- Psychotherapy
- Group Therapy
- Collaboration between Royal College of Psychiatrists and press to present realistic pictures of human health and beauty

## Case history - Fiona

'It seems hard to believe it looking back after 18 months on the ward. I mean, I was literally a walking skeleton. Mum showed me photos they had taken. I weighed 5 stones and all I could see was this out-of-control fat person! Jesus.

You know what finally turned things? It was Janine, my roommate on the Ward. They said I could say goodbye before the Undertaker came. There was the bed and this rumpled sheet. I thought they had taken her but was curious and looked under the sheet. I couldn't stop vomiting. Suddenly, I was scared.'

Fiona walked slowly into the office and smiled wanly. I tried to hide my shock. Just behind the thin skin I could see the outline of her skull, a vague circular blueness around the hollowed eyes, the high points of bone protruding from her skin, her teeth yellowish and mottled. It was at variance with the picture her mother showed me of Fiona at 10 years a happy, smiling child. She noticed my shock and looked puzzled.

This was a young woman of 26, recently married with a kind husband and caring parents. She had a steady job and enjoyed activities outside work including painting and clubbing. She was looking forward to having children of her own and only agreed to see her General Practitioner as her menstrual cycle had stopped.

He took one look, listened to her refusal to stay into Hospital then called the Hospital Social Worker. Fiona was sectioned. She was too weak to offer resistance but kept repeating there was nothing wrong only her periods.

Dr Redding warned me that Fiona was physically low but I've never seen anyone that emaciated still alive. The hardest bit was trying not to stare. Fiona wasn't abused or deprived. I talked to her for weeks. She had loving parents, friends, a boyfriend, a job. She told me these things sitting with her feet curled under her.

We started to talk about weight. She hadn't minded talking about her feelings but the minute I mentioned weight I noticed her thin hands gripping a chair, her tongue darted about dry lips.

On the Ward Fiona was weighed every day and when meals arrived one of the Mental Nurses would sit with her to make sure she did not hide or vomit food. Fiona was cunning. When the Nurses weren't looking she told me how the Ward plants and toilet cisterns received regular doses of squashed up food. She had even hidden food in her slippers, flushing it down the toilet later. Luckily the Nurses were wise to these deadly games.

It was months before I managed to get through. It was after her friend Janine died. Janine was 22 and weighed 4½ stones. Fiona was quiet, subdued. She started talking about how sometimes people might see things that weren't right; not hallucinations– just, *sort of narrowing things down a bit* as she put it.

We began to talk more. About magazines and that there were only six Supermodels out of the whole population. We talked about getting

154

older and she said that was scary. We talked on and on, about feelings and this and that. We never talked specifically about Fiona's weight or Fiona's food. We just came to an understanding. One day she blurted out about the rape. After that, things got easier.

Sadly she split up with her boyfriend. He could not cope with the emotional strain. I discharged her two years later. I remember her waving, walking down the drive to the Hospital, hand in hand with her mother. She was still slight, an adult girl. She was elfin like with the huge eyes of an African child. But there was a small glow about her and a little spring in her step. And you know what I felt I was losing a daughter. Of those who entered hospital with her – Jamie, Esther, Sally, June, Marina and Nadine, only Fiona and Marina were still alive.

\*\*\*\*\*\*\*\*\*\*

## Mania

Many of our finest creatives (artists, writers, poets) have been diagnosed with mania or manic-depressive illness. Mania is characterised by periods of intensive activity, rapid bursts of energy and irrational thinking. The moods are opposite to those of depressive illness. The illness can manifest alone or more commonly with depression (bi-polar or MDP).

High and happy are not the same thing. There are elements of happiness, extreme happiness - but overshadowed by fear of this out-of-control state. Think of times when you have laughed, loud and long and then imagine you need to stop laughing but can't. Your muscles are aching, everyone has had enough but you just can't stop.

Manic people can be fun to be with until the mood swings so high it becomes embarrassing. As with depressive illness a manic attack cannot be controlled. The brain chemistry is firing at speed and only medication can reduce the extreme to normality. It is only later that the cost of destructive behaviour such as excessive spending or promiscuous activity comes home.

## Links to Depression

People who suffer depressive illness are, to a greater or lesser degree, prone to attacks of mania when they swing out of low mood. It is almost a reaction which says that was hellish I'm going to make darned sure it doesn't happen again. From being depressed, the chemistry overcompensates and moves into mania.

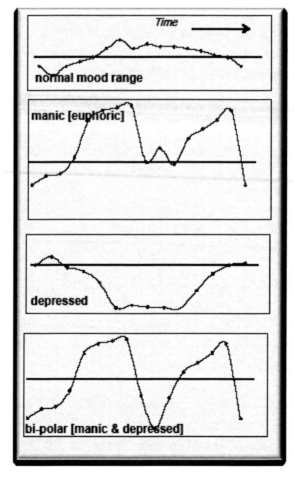

# Bi - Polar Illness

This is a common variation, the sufferer going from depressed to manic in varying cycles. The moods swing from one extreme to the other in cycles of varying duration. The swings can be erratic, of long or short duration or with long lengths of time between *episodes.*

## SYMPTOMS
Physical
- Increase in energy ('psychomotor agitation')
- Marked increase in activity levels
- Decreased need for sleep

Mental
- Patient highly inflated opinion of him/her self (grandiosity)
- Very talkative
- Lack of concentration
- May indulge in promiscuous activity, or unwise investing

Causes
- Imbalance of brain chemistry
- Family history of the illness (genetic factors)
- Over reaction to recovery from depression
- Abuse of alcohol or drugs

## Attitudes
Mania is relatively uncommon. People might tolerate what can be perceived as euphoria unless the behaviour relates to a dangerous situation, e.g. driving, trying to jump off a high building in the belief they are invincible, trying to set light to a building under a delusion.

Radio DJ Kenny Everett was frequently hospitalized for mania yet was acknowledged as one of the most creative DJ's of his generation. Kay Redfield Jamison's *Touched With Fire* is an excellent book on the subject of creativity, genius and mania.

## Cures/ Remedies

- Medications which change the brain chemistry
- Psycho Analysis - *used before the advent of medication*
- Behavioural Therapy

## Case History - Emma

'I've been coming down over the last day or so. I enjoy the mood when it comes on. There's no warning just a buzzy feeling like champagne bubbles in my blood. Things start to get better. The world is colourful. Even the grass is brighter and greenier. Do you like that, greenier? That's a word I invented when I was high. I feel a tremendous burst of energy and you know I feel I can do anything!'

'I went shopping last time' (*she points to her wardrobe, which is bursting at the seams with colourful clothing*). 'Look at that lot! The credit card company was furious. It took months and I'm still paying it off. But wow! I remember how it felt in the shop. Everyone was looking and I was really enjoying myself. God, just like mother!' She looks uncomfortable and wriggles in her chair.

'After a few days I start to get sweaty. I know the mood is overtaking me and I can't control it. My voice gets higher and louder and I grit my teeth but there's nothing I can do. I just jabber on and on and get ideas.' She looks suddenly embarrassed.

'And I keep picking up men. One night stands. Sometimes more than one. It's great at first then I get uncomfortable. But it goes on and they get scared and leave. Then I shout. I really want to sleep but I can't and keep pacing the room. I feel used and dirty.' She breaks off into loud sobs. After a minute or so she visibly brightens and rubs her face.

'But, well, it's good at the time. The moods are rapid though I get dog-tired. Up then down. Not depressed you know but normal mood for me is being down. It's all or nothing. Yes, it's exhausting. I can't stop whatever I'm doing. And the money I've spent! God, I must have wasted thousands on junk that seemed marvellous at the time. No wonder shopkeepers love me'.

'I call myself Esmerelda when I'm high. Esmerelda the gypsy [from the novel, *The Hunchback of Notre Dame*]. Do you like it?' She doesn't wait for an answer but starts to get excited.

'Sanctuary! Do you remember Charles Laughton? I imagine myself swinging from the rope into the Cathedral! What fun! The Queen went to the Premier. I really wanted to meet her. I am sure she would have liked me. I nearly met her once at a Garden Party. Gosh, I should have been an actress when I was younger.'

She breaks off, fetches a glass of water and a bottle of pills. She opens the bottle and dramatically swallows two.

'There. I need them but it's hard to remember. It's Lithium. Balances the mood. Supposed to. Look at that.' She holds out her hand which is shaking visibly. 'Been like that for years. God, I feel old!' She looks in the mirror, sighs and plumps down in her chair. Big tears start to roll down her cheeks.

'I do feel really, really old. It's like I've lived two lives and not enjoyed one of them. And I know they make fun of me – think I'm an old drama queen and laugh behind my back. But honestly Marianne it they only knew what it was really like. I'm scared inside and exhausted'.

'I feel like the girl with magic dancing shoes. I can't stop. Oh, sometimes I just wish I was normal, just for a while.'

She sinks into her chair and I, unable to say anything, sit and almost feel her exhaustion. I try to imagine what her relatives must be suffering too.

## Obsessive Compulsive Disorder (OCD)

We all might check doors are locked before going out but when this checking gets out of order it becomes a crippling illness. The obsessions [about the thing or idea] lead to a compulsion (ritual or task) to alleviate the obsession. Rituals, like religious rituals, tend to bring comfort and ward off potential disaster. The person is aware of what they are doing but can neither control the action nor explain it.

OCD can be long-standing. Obsessive people are orderly to an excessive degree. It is not common occurring in only 1.5 to 2% of people in a year. Not much is known about this illness which is attributed to genetic factors and chemical imbalances. It is difficult to cure although CBT and medication both help.

## Obsessions, Compulsions, and Rituals

This unusual disorder has three common elements:

**Obsession** – a fixated idea which cannot be stopped
**Compulsion** – an uncontrollable urge or belief
**Ritual** – rigid procedures in a specific order

## Orderliness

People with Obsessive-Compulsive Disorder (OCD) are over organised. Objects are regimentally laid out. It is as if they cannot tolerate disorganisation. The compulsion to make things orderly is not under their control. Neither can they stop before completion of the tasks they have set themselves.

## SYMPTOMS

Mental – Obsessions
1   Persistent ideas – e.g. their house is contaminated
2   Persistent thoughts – burglars are going to raid their home
3   Persistent images – crude sexual imagery

Physical – Compulsions
1    constant hand washing, (sometimes until the skin bleeds)
2    repeated checking and testing of locks and doors
3    constant praying to try to negate guilt feelings

Causes:
- Imbalance in brain chemistry
- Trauma
- Genetic factors

## Cures/ Remedies
OCD is sometimes treated with medication. It has no known cure but can be controlled with medication and psychological treatment.

Patients are given a programme of CBT designed to reduce the amount of time spent doing the ritual. At the same time the patient receives counselling designed to try to help him/her deal with the original obsession and discover its cause.

## Case History - Cynthia
Walking into Cynthia's home was like walking into a show house. Nothing was out of place, not a speck of dust. She perched on the edge of a rather uncomfortable-looking leather chesterfield wearing a neat navy suit of old-fashioned kind. Her immaculate hair was lacquered in place, every detail of makeup perfect. Nevertheless as we spoke I noticed her glancing regularly into a large mirror on the opposite wall brushing imaginary stray hairs.

'I first started this." she gestured helplessly with her hand, 'this, well, cleaning a year ago. At first, I wasn't aware of what I was doing. Marjorie my daily help kept asking if I wanted to dispense with her services. I asked why. She said there didn't seem to be a need. I told her that the house needed a deep clean and that she might have an extra day for the extra work.'

Cynthia paused then managed a smile. 'Well, she was an honest woman. After a week she sat me down on the sofa and asked me to look around. Gradually I took in her meaning. I had spent literally all day on my hands and knees rubbing every spot of dirt from the carpet then an hour scrubbing my hands. My hands were raw and the skin between the fingers bleeding.

Cynthia sat looking at her hands then looked at me. 'Of course, it started soon after my husband Geoff, died. He died of a chest infection.' She paused again and I nodded. She gestured with her hands unable to speak.

'So' I said 'Perhaps you wanted to scrub away memories as if it hadn't happened?'

'I feel it was more to do with blaming myself really. As if the cleaning could work a kind of magic and bring him back. A ritual.' She sat thinking. After a few minutes I interrupted.

'And now?'

'Now' she replied, 'I can't control it. I know what I am doing but I can't help myself.' At that point a red-faced kindly looking woman opened the door. Marjorie. I looked at the two women.

'Perhaps Marjorie can be a part of this programme. We will be doing something very different to your usual practice Marjorie. It will involve not cleaning, encouraging dirt'.

Marjorie smiled. 'Right. Shall we start with tea?' Cynthia laughed.

\*\*\*\*\*\*\*\*\*\*

## Personality Disorders

There are many types of personality disorder. The most widely known is the extreme, psychopathic personality disorder. Murders committed by psychopathic serial killers make highly saleable news. However, there are many less devastating types which are amenable to therapy, although there is no known cure.

Not everyone will be diagnosed because there are many pathological but ordinary people living in the community. The obvious criteria for those who attend treatment is how far the person is able to stabilise without intervention. There are aspects of personality disorder in everyone; cruelty, mocking, goading, bullying are in human nature and it is only morality or conscience which stops these turning into evil action. In the most severe forms, such as psychopathic personality disorder, the conscience does not exist nor can one be artificially introduced.

It is not only a genetic condition but also driven by upbringing and life circumstances. Recent evidence seems to point this way. In many cases of personality disorder there is a background of cruelty and abuse stretching throughout childhood. Sufferers repeat behaviour ingrained in their genes; these are the wife or husband batterers; hysterical; socially isolated; murderous, unable to control the impulses which others might resist.

As patients, people with enduring personality disorder can be hard to understand, difficult to treat. They are not likeable people but this is out of their control.

Where do they go? What do they do for a living? For those on the very edge the dirtiest jobs, the most dangerous, ones where human contact is not a daily feature. For others they will experience great difficulty holding down jobs and suffer enormous anxiety. Without relations to care or friends to be tolerant, the prognosis is not good admittedly. Science is not yet prepared for this disorder, although one day it will most likely be through genetic re-engineering.

## SYMPTOMS

These disorders are divided into types each with its particular characteristic.

General features:
- individual behaves in a markedly different way to others
- experiences problems over a wide range of behaviours
- the condition is of long standing

Physical
- No marked physical symptoms.

Types
- Anti social – shuns people and society
- Avoidant - inhibited
- Borderline – impulsive; difficulties in forming relationships
- Dependent – submissive and clinging
- Narcissistic – self obsessed
- Paranoid - distrustful
- Psychopathic – highly destructive; unaware of their illness
- Schizoid – withdrawing and detached

Causes:
- Genetic factors
- Dysfunctional home life from early age

Cures/ Remedies
- no cure
- medication can control some symptoms
- hospitalisation
- Electro Convulsive therapy
- Psychotherapy
- Cognitive-Behavioural Therapy

**Case History – Tom**

'Never been married, me. I knew since I were a boy I would be on my tod. If you told me I would still be alone at 50 in this place – grim aint it? I'd have topped myself. Thought about that a lot I have.'

He drags deep on a roll up and blows smoke at the ceiling which is cracked and yellow with a suggestion of brown ooze. An iron bedstead covered in grubby bedding sags in a corner. A cheap utility wardrobe and dressing table with a cracked mirror and two wooden chairs, the ones we are sitting on, are the only other furniture.

'I don't really know why you're here. Yea, it's alright, as long as you don't stop too long. Can't stand company. I expect they told you that.' He drags again and coughs. 'What was it like? You mean working? Ah.'

'Couldn't settle. One job after another– stores work, janitor, *on the track*, van deliveries, day labourer. Always some cocky bastard or boring lout got to me in the end and started a fight. I dunno'. He seems puzzled, rubs his chin and stares at the floor.

'Wanted to stay. Changing jobs is tiring. I'm getting on. Week here, month there – whole year once! Always in the end there's one. I deck 'em or run at 'em. Get me cards. Always the same. Parents? Pop was ex-army – Corporal. Corporal Punishment I called him when I was a lad!' We share the joke as he laughs and coughs.

'Great believer in the strap, backhand to the face and a stream of ... Friends? Na. No one was allowed. Mother? Little timid bitch. Mousey. Didn't think much of her. Love?' He laughs bitterly. For a second I think he is going to cry but he controls it, spits and drags on the wet end of his roll-up.

'He used to land her one regular. Stop him? What for? That's what a wife's about, ain't it? When I was older used to land her one meself. That's how it is.'

'As a kid? Never one for games, never joined in. Wanted to– but, its hard you know. I used to watch how the others did it – sort of sidling up then getting in the game. You know what kids are. Cruel bastards. They'd run off if I get up to them.'

'What did I do?' he laughs harshly. 'bash 'em. I was known for it. Proud? I'll say– it was the only thing I had, me fists. Dad would have been proud.' A tinge of regret in his voice. 'Well, he died see so he never knew. Going? Now? Well you'll come again mebbe... if I'm in' He coughs, follows me to the door.

As I walk down the drive I see he is watching from the other side of the grubby nets. I know he will never admit it but he dreads the years ahead. He knows something is wrong but doesn't know what to do. He is too proud to ask. I know he won't allow me in very often. There will be an excuse. Occasionally, he might, to alleviate the loneliness. I suspect in the end he will jump in front of the train, as he said he might.

**********

## Phobia

Phobias are excessive fears about objects, things or situations. They are fears or anxieties about anything – it could be going out, an animal, blood and needles, flying. They prevent the sufferer living a normal life. This condition is fairly common, occurring among about 10 – 11% of the population.

Phobias start out specific i.e. fear of a single item, then fear of other things which resemble that item, then the fear spreads to encompass a whole range of similar things.

## SYMPTOMS

Physical
- No particular physical symptoms.

Mental

- Excessive or unreasonable fear of object, thing, or place
- Avoidance of situation where they would have to face fear
- Daily living is affected to a marked degree
- The fear is of long standing

*See diagram overleaf.*

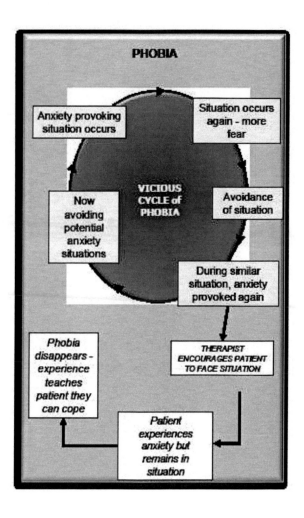

## Common Phobias

- Agora – fear of open spaces
- Arachna – fear of spiders
- Blood/infection – fear of being contaminated
- Claustro – fear of being in a confined space
- Obsessional Compulsive Disorder
- Post traumatic Stress Disorder (PTSD) –after major accident
  Situational – fear of a situation  e.g. flying, spiders, blood
- Social – fear of social situations

Causes

- Excessive reaction to one or more negative incidents connected with the phobia
- Worsening of an existing fear – e.g. fear of spiders
- Reaction to loss – e.g. leading to excessive fear of dying
- Reaction to incident which occurred in distant past

Cures/ Remedies

- Behavioural therapy
- Psychotherapy
- Cognitive-Behavioural therapy

Phobias are treatable using behaviour therapy or systematic desensitivisation. The therapist will encourage the sufferer to face the situation they have been avoiding, but in a controlled way over weeks or months. Or a talking therapy might be used to discover the root or source of the phobia.

### Case history - Mike

'I'm sorry I couldn't answer the door. It's getting worse in the last few weeks. Then, I could have got to the garden gate without faintness coming on. How long? I've been confined in the house for 8 months. I last went out in January with Mary (his wife) for the sales.'

He is neatly dressed, the house is bright and clean. But he has moved his bed into the lounge and it seems he is only living in one room.

'It's odd. If you'd told me a year ago I would be afraid to walk outside my own front door I could never have believed it. Neither would Mary.' He pauses, remembering.

'It started at Mary's funeral. I got out of the car and looked at the trees – I started to feel faint. The trees seemed to be coming in on me. I put it down to grief. It all went off alright. Plenty of our friends turned up to say goodbye to her. After, we walked back to the cars and I was feeling very dizzy. I was glad to get inside.'

'After that, it was a succession of things. At first, it was just going to town. It's about three miles and I usually drove us both. We would have a bite to eat in a café halfway and so I did the same – on my own.'

'The dizziness came back and a wave of anxiety. The first time I rushed back to the car then I drove home and it was ok.'

'A few times after that I had to leave the Supermarket. I was at the check out queue when I just had to leave. I can't really tell you why, it was a sort of panic.'

'After that it got worse gradually until I had to shop locally just around the corner. At least I could leave quickly without anyone noticing. And me a man! I was so embarrassed I couldn't tell anyone. I always thought this was a woman's thing'.

'Well eventually I could only get to the garden gate before this wave of anxiety came over me and I had to turn back. I'd tell myself it was ridiculous but that made no difference. Each time I panicked and that made it worse next time.'

'I thought if I stayed in the house it would wear off. So I found a home help to do the shopping and moved everything into this room so I could avoid going out.'

He looks really embarrassed, and with a voice tinged with anxiety, says: 'Is there any hope that I'll get over this? I couldn't bear being confined like this for the rest of my life. It's almost as if I'm in a coffin, like Mary.' He bursts into tears.

We persisted for several weeks starting with him walking halfway up his drive. I walked behind him until he was able to get in his car. Eventually, he could do the journey alone, while I waited in his house. After that, he agreed to go for bereavement counselling and things just improved from there.

\*\*\*\*\*\*\*\*\*\*

## Schizophrenia

Schizophrenia is a much misunderstood illnesses even among medical people who argue its cluster of disparate symptoms. It is not split personality. Schizophrenia is marked by perceptual disturbances, leading to delusions and hallucinations which appear real to the patient but cannot be seen by anyone else. In this way, it can be frightening for both patient and observers. Visual and aural disturbances interfere with how the patient perceives the real world. Hallucinations and voices do not always manifest as destructive or evil. These can take the form of religious images, or cartoon characters. Artists with this illness can be highly creative. There are many disparate symptoms which do not manifest at the same time or in the same way. Patients display no emotion or excessive emotion.

The film *A Beautiful Mind* unfolds the story of US mathematician Dr John Nash who developed schizophrenia before the advent of medication. Dr Nash was treated with ECT and later with new medications as they were developed. Although he never fully recovered his faculties nevertheless he married, had a son and was able to continue working informally at mathematical problems eventually winning a Nobel Prize. The film cleverly demonstrates the delusions and hallucinations which are a hallmark of this illness.

A very few patients with schizophrenia who fail to take medication can become a danger to the public. Pre-medication, these are the patients who would have been confined in an Asylum. Where murders are committed by these very ill patients, it is under the powerful influence of delusions, not that these acts are being done deliberately.

About 1% of the population is affected by one of these disorders which generally begin during adolescence although (rarely) manifests from middle age. Many patients with schizophrenia who continue taking their antipsychotic medication can lead relatively normal lives.

## Diagnosis and Cultural Factors

This illness needs careful diagnosis. Disturbances of vision and hearing can be drug induced. Some cultures are tolerant of and encourage factors which in Western culture would lead to a diagnosis of hallucinations and delusions:

- religious ecstasies in which spiritual images are seen
- speaking in tongues
- ancestors appear to the living and advise them
- spiritualists, communicate with the dead
- artists speak figuratively of what he/she intend to create

## Stigma

Schizophrenia carries huge stigma, the result of stories of psychotic killers. These people do exist but are very few in number. Social effects are devastating with patients who are unable to hold down a job or unable to access support then drift down the social scale. In the 1990's many prisoners were ex-Asylum patients unable to cope with life in the community.

## SYMPTOMS

The symptoms must be of at least 6 months standing. If you compare symptoms with those of Brief Psychotic Disorder, you will notice similarities, although the former is of shorter term.

Physical
- Sufferers may show signs of a lack of personal self care

Mental
- Delusions – persistent irrational thoughts
- Hallucinations – seeing or hearing things that are not there
- Speech can be meaningless (word salad)
- No feelings are apparent
- Behaviour disorganised or non-existent (*catatonic*)

Types
- Catatonic– rigid, repeated actions, no stimulation
- Paranoid – one or more powerful delusions of extreme fear

### Catatonia

Now relatively rare, this type of schizophrenia has the effect of stupefying the individual who sits in an almost permanent comatose state. I remember a lady in a Scottish Asylum who sat in the same chair for years, taking meals on her chair and never speaking or moving. One student nurse made considerable efforts to talk to her and the woman started to respond only to sink back when this nurse left.

### Paranoid

A type of schizophrenia where delusions (false beliefs) centre on a powerful delusion.

This form can be dangerous when voices are threatening and evil and suggest the patient commits murder.

## Confusion with Psychopathic Personality Disorder

Paranoid schizophrenia may be confused with Psychopathic Personality Disorder. A Psychopath is born without conscience and is therefore unable to distinguish between right and wrong acts. Someone with schizophrenia is able to make distinctions but acts under powerful delusions which mask reality.

Causes
- Generally attributed to one or more of the following:
- Family history of the illness
- Traumatic childhood/ family events

Treatments
- Medications which change brain chemistry
- Behavioural Therapy, in conjunction with medication
- Living in a Therapeutic Community

This illness cannot be cured but can be controlled with medication. There are many people with schizophrenia living and working in the Community with their symptoms controlled with medication. Medication alleviates psychotic symptoms.

However, under the influence of delusions, some patients believe medication is poison being administered and refuse to take it or refuse treatment. It is these patients who can become a social or legal hazard.

## Case History - Mandy

Mandy is a bright, intelligent girl of 26 who was diagnosed with schizophrenia when she was 15. She lives alone in a small flat and receives irregular visits from her parents and a once a week visit from a Rehabilitation Therapist.

After her breakdown she had to leave her Business Studies course because she was unable to cope with the intellectual demands. Her boyfriend left her when she was diagnosed and since then she has had no relationships.

'Of course I feel sad about not being able to work only in a sheltered scheme as the images are intrusive and sometimes the voices so loud I can't concentrate. I know I will never do the things I set out to do, Business Management, and that grieves me. I want to be ordinary but I know there is no cure. It took years to accept that.'

'How did I realize something was wrong? I didn't notice; my parents did. I started shutting myself off, I don't really know why, except it was difficult to concentrate and I kept feeling fuzziness in my head as if there was cotton-wool inside my brain.'

'Then one day I was on a boat on the Thames looking over at the buildings on the other side. A sort of gash appeared in the sky as if it was a painting and someone had ripped a great piece of it out and there were bizarre figures in the rip. I couldn't make it out. I turned to tell my friend and there was this horrible look of shock on her face – she couldn't see it apparently. That scared me.'

'After that things started to get worse. I started hearing voices. I couldn't see their bodies but they were very real. No one else could hear them; I assumed they could at first, like the picture thing, but I couldn't bear the reactions when I told people, so I kept it to myself. I was just so lonely.'

'My College work was suffering. I had been working really hard for the exams – perhaps too hard. It was impossible to concentrate with all these weird things going on. I knew I was getting insane but was trying to ignore it.'

'One day I heard a voice saying the boy next to me was going to kill me. I turned to look at him. I could see his face changing. His face sort of started to melt. Apparently, I grabbed an art knife and tried to stab him. That's when they called someone and I was taken into hospital.'

'It was such a relief to talk about what I was seeing and the voices. The Doctor seemed to understand and nodded as if it were an everyday occurrence. I suppose it was to him. Anyway, it made me feel better.'

'I asked him if I was mad and he said that madness was a term ignorant people used to describe something they couldn't understand and were frightened of. He said I had schizophrenia and that it could be controlled with medication.'

'I told him I was really scared, that I didn't mean to harm that boy and I didn't want to be locked away. I asked him if I would be put away and he said that as long as I took the medication things would be fine. He told me someone from the Community Mental Health Team would visit me regularly to make sure everything was OK.'

'I sort of got very lonely especially as my parents rarely visit. I know they are upset but they are also afraid. I suppose it's easier for them not to come. They couldn't cope with me at home all the time, sitting around, and talking to my voices.'

'I believe mum's sister had this too, so I suppose it brings it all back to them. Tom, the boy I tried to stab, visits me. I feel really guilty but he knows I believed the voices – and they haven't come back since I started taking my medication.'

'He doesn't seem to mind the flat being messy. I can't get it together to clean very often as I get confused. I kind of hope he visits more often.'

**********

# Chapter 12

## Social & Complementary Approaches

**Content of this Chapter:**
Social Interpretation
Harmony of Mind, Body, and Spirit
Complementary Practitioners
Spiritual Pursuits
Yoga

If I asked you to get into a locked house you might consider several approaches - a key, breaking a window, taking the putty out of the glass, climbing over a fence at the back, shinning up a drainpipe. Some might be effective, others destructive or even dangerous. How you chose to get in would depend upon circumstances. For instance, if there was a fire and children screaming at the windows. Likewise, there are many ways of approaching the alleviation of mental illness.

Research shows there to be effective treatments outside medicine for non-psychotic symptoms and there is also anecdotal evidence that some complementary treatments offer respite, relaxation and reduction of fear.

For the purposes of this chapter, be aware these interpretations do not refer to psychotic symptoms which are best treated with hospitalisation and medication. Although psychotic symptoms can very rarely pass without medication, extensive personal trauma is involved which might damage the *psyche*.

There are many theories other than genetics to explain the causes of mental illness, some of them covered in the section on the history of mental illness. Cause necessarily dictates the method used for cure, or alleviation. For those with mild to moderate depression, anxiety and other trauma, environmental and holistic theories can work very well in practice, although it is good to remember that there are as many rogues in the complementaries as there are in the medical professions.

## Social Interpretation

The social theory of mental illness holds that there is no such thing as mental illness but only problems of relationships between people in close societies. Given love, support and understanding the theory goes, people will thrive and be tolerated no matter what behaviours they display. Under these circumstances there will supposedly be little anti-social behaviour (*so goes this theory*). Read the writing of Psychiatrist R D Laing who has written extensively on the myth of mental illness.

We have only to look at the so-called primitive cultures where ancestors are revered. What we term psychotic symptoms are perceived as manifestations of good ancestral spirits. Therefore, those who show such symptoms are not carted off to hospital but are revered and looked after in the Community. This type of attitude must surely be a positive pattern. However it is impossible to draft one culture with its ideas and long standing beliefs onto another.

## Harmony of Mind, Body, and Spirit

Most prevalent among holistic therapists is the belief that mental health and physical health [mind and body] affect each other. Therefore treatment of one will have a beneficial effect upon the other.

Imagine you have a cold; does it affect how you feel and think? However, if you are well and the sun is shining conversely does that affect your mental state? It is possible to be both physically well and mentally unstable, disabled yet cheerful, physically sound but sour. Mind can often transcend physical circumstances.

## BALANCED PERSONALITY [*holism*]

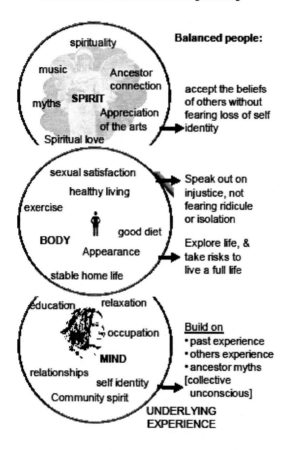

**Balanced people:**

spirituality

music

Ancestor connection

myths **SPIRIT**

Appreciation of the arts

Spiritual love

accept the beliefs of others without fearing loss of self identity

sexual satisfaction

healthy living

exercise

**BODY**

good diet

Appearance

stable home life

Speak out on injustice, not fearing ridicule or isolation

Explore life, & take risks to live a full life

education    relaxation

occupation

**MIND**

relationships

self identity

Community spirit

Build on
• past experience
• others experience
• ancestor myths
[collective unconscious]

UNDERLYING EXPERIENCE

### Benefits of a Balanced Personality

The mind/body/spirit or holistic approach theory proposes these three states in harmony, brings a happy life despite considerations of any kind of disability.

With harmony of mind, body, spirit, anyone can achieve. They will be at peace with themselves and the community, find themselves with energy they can devote to just causes. Refer to the diagram overleaf.

**Mind** – relating, suitable occupation, identity, ability to relax
**Body** – physical health and appearance
**Spirit** - ability to perceive beauty, art, spiritual experience

### Stages of Life

In all primitive cultures there exist rites of passage. At certain critical times in a human being's existence, important stages have to be successfully achieved before the next stage is reached:

- birth
- age 5 – going to school
- age 13 – puberty
- aged 18 – entering adulthood
- age 40's – mid life
- age 80's – old age
- ++ - advanced old age

I am sure we all recognise instances of *puer eternis* or eternal youth, a man who never grows up or the spiteful gossip who lives to a lonely old age. Rituals are marked with ceremonies throughout the world but in Western culture these are less likely to be physical challenges so much as dressing up in best clothing, consuming food and alcohol, receiving congratulatory cards.

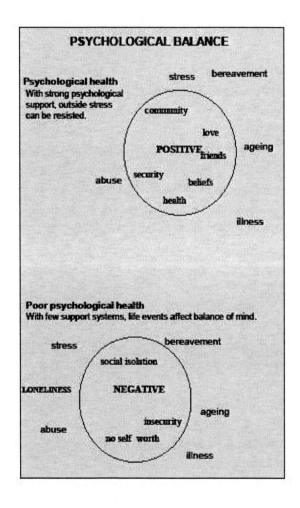

Where a mental age block is reached, a Therapist's task is to help their client out of the stuck stage. Jungians (followers of Carl Jung) specialize in the important passage through the middle years towards maturity (*individuation*).

## Complementary Practitioners

Complementary or holistic therapies - the word depends upon your preference. These therapists work on the level of mind, body and spirit.

There are more complementary therapies than I have room for in this brief chapter, including an interesting Humour Therapy clinic currently being set up in the USA by Dr Patch Adams, whose appeal for staff received responses from huge numbers of medically trained professionals in the US (the film *Patch Adams* explores Patch's story).

Alternative or complementaries are useful not only for patients but also relatives and friends who suffer the distress of helping a loved one through with an episode of mental illness. Not all of these suit everyone and not all of them are proven. It is wise not to spend a lot of money until sure of the chosen therapy and Therapist. There are many charlatans in the complementary field.

From creative writing and art therapies through Eastern philosophy (Chinese medicine, reflexology) to what has is now mainstream (acupuncture, herbalists, aromatherapy, chiropractic) there is something to suit every philosophy of life.

In the East there is a saying, when the pupil is ready a suitable teacher emerges. One of the curiosities of life is that this often happens.

## Aromatherapy/Massage

Aromatherapy is a body massage in which the Therapist uses scented natural plant and mineral oils to treat specific disorders. Plants are the forerunners of 25% of medications we use. Those synthesised in laboratories assure *parity* (quality) and a considerable amount of research has gone into proving plants to be effective for specific symptoms. In the West we discovered this recently. The Chinese have known it for thousands of years.

Aromatherapy is very relaxing. Once the body is relaxed, the appropriate oils seep deeply into the body and the mind begins to drift. This is an excellent therapy for those who do not like talking about problems. It provides caring, physical contact without the stress of being psychologically naked. For the shy, masseurs (male) and masseuse (female) are good with strategically placing towels so clients do not feel embarrassed.

## Reflexology

A similar therapy for those who do not find physical contact easy is Reflexology. This therapy is a dry massage using talcum powder on the feet or the hands.

Reflexology works on the principal that the body has meridian lines running through it in vertical lines, each line connecting areas of energy. When there is a blockage along one of the lines which correspond to the body organs the line runs through, that causes pain. The Reflexologist's job is to find areas of blockage and release them through massage, thus restoring the body to harmony.

Reflexology has been used in China for thousands of years and also in Egypt. A scene is depicted on a famous tomb wall painting. The patient says '*do not hurt me*' and the practitioner replies '*I shall act so that you will praise me*'. The practitioner is depicted working on the toes of his patient. This theory underlies much of the Chinese medicine system, which works on the harmony or Tao of body and mind.

## Art Therapies

Originally considered fringe there are many taking to art therapies of all kinds.

183

In art painting therapy the patient is given media (crayon, paint, chalk) with which to draw. The idea is not be to create a technical masterpiece but allow the emotions to be expressed. When the piece is finished the Therapist discusses the meaning of the drawing with the patient. There are many types of art therapy; poetry, reading, psychodrama. Patients in Psychiatric Hospitals are always encouraged to take part in art therapy.

Psychodrama involves the client or patient acting out incidents from their past almost as if in a play. Interpretations and alternative scenarios can be explored in what can be intense but enlightening sessions.

The only difference between art and art conducted as therapy is that the latter involves psychological interpretation. Certainly writing, drawing, and reading are excellent ways of de-stressing, whether or not they are formal therapy.

## Reichian Therapy

Reichian therapy is less commonly practiced. Wilhelm Reich proposed that during times of mental torment the bodily systems literally lock, preventing a person from moving in a normal manner. If the body is unlocked then the physical body returns to harmony and is released from mental tension.

## Chiropractic/Osteopathy

Chiropractic is designed to restore health by manipulating the spine by hand. The aim is to re-align joints which have become misplaced through bad posture and freeing nerves which have become trapped. It is a similar theoretical stance to Reichian Therapy. Often when someone is undergoing stress or crisis situations they start to hold themselves differently; hunch, cringe, curl.

Even in normal working conditions with a large proportion of the population working with computers, posture becomes bad through poor siting of equipment. Driving can seriously misalign the body particularly the neck and spine.

Less gentle but none-the-less as effective is osteopathy. An osteopath makes sharper physical adjustments which can be disconcerting to the beginner.

### Crystal Therapy

Natural minerals are beautiful to look at but this therapy proposes that the crystals emit vibrations which can be used to heal various aspects of illness. Each type of crystal supposedly works on a specific wavelength and heals a different problem.

Not a therapy I recommend from personal use but for the pure pleasure of handling these lovely minerals. It is relaxing looking at and feeling them.

Do not spend large amounts of money on crystals at healing conventions; you can purchase them more cheaply online.

### Spiritual Pursuits

Books on Taoism or Buddhism are not the dry tomes you might expect and contain enlightening information. Sufi tales make very interesting reading. These are a kind of allegory.

Try also *The Miracle of Mindfulness* by Thich Nhat Hanh (Tich Nat Han); simple daily practices to bring peace into your life that make the most mundane of tasks enjoyable. Taoists are renowned for peaceful demeanor and sense of humour. The practice of mindfulness is growing even among NHS practitioners.

Any of the mainstream religious practices can bring spiritual relief but need to be practiced sincerely. Most recommend prayer or meditation can be uplifting when experienced in large groups of like minded people.

The value is not only in individual practice but the power of others sharing this most mystical of experiences. Beyond both words and touch, spiritual practice is good for anyone with mental turmoil particularly those who find physical contact difficult.

## Yoga

For those who prefer something a little more physical there is Yoga, a watered down Western version of the incredible exercises practiced by Yogis (spiritual teachers) in India.

Yoga is exercise and meditation in one and promotes physical and mental health, whilst also promoting suppleness of body. One 91 year-old friend of mine remained supple thanks to taking up yoga at the ripe age of 64 years.

There are many versions, some very physical and consisting of complex postures. Or there is the less taxing hatha form which concentrates on breathing techniques to free the spirit.

Those around someone with mental illness are often neglected even though they often bear the brunt of the care of their loved one. Spiritual practices and complementary therapies should not be underestimated for their positive effects on mind and body. There is a great deal of information on these therapies but steer clear of the charlatans.

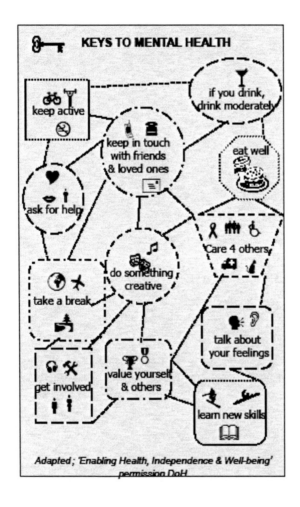

KEYS TO MENTAL HEALTH

if you drink, drink moderately

keep active

keep in touch with friends & loved ones

eat well

ask for help

Care 4 others

do something creative

take a break

talk about your feelings

get involved

value yourself & others

learn new skills

Adapted; 'Enabling Health, Independence & Well-being' permission DoH

187

# Chapter 13

## Reflections

---

### Sayings to uplift the spirits

If you are too busy to read whole books, brief sayings or *affirmations* are a very useful psychological bolster in times of difficulty. There are many collections available on the Internet or in bookshops. Copy your favourites so that they will be on hand for the next time you need an uplift.

Here are a few of ideas I have collected over the years and some of my own. I hope you enjoy reading them. I often buy books from second-hand shops and some of the authors may not be well known to the reader of modern literature. However there is much excellent material and it is uncanny how you might recognise how later authors obtained inspiration from the same well of knowledge.

### Community and Responsibility

'Where one member suffers, all the members suffer with it'
**St Paul**

'Our smallest actions may affect profoundly the whole lives of people who have nothing to do with us.'
**Somerset Maughan**

'The worm that destroys you is the temptation to agree with your critics to get their approval'
**'Hannibal' Thomas Harris**

'I am a part of all that I have met,
Yet all experience is an arch wherethro gleams
The untravelled world whose margin fades forever
When I move.'
**'Ulysses' by Alfred Lord Tennyson**

## Death and Survival

'Things are both more trivial and more important than they ever were... the nowness of everything is absolutely wondrous.'
**Dennis Potter** – *shortly before his death from cancer*

'Whoso can look on death, will start at no shadow.'
**Greek saying**

'When you hear that the individual with the warmest heart and deepest piety ...ended in a gas chamber, then you either go and hang yourself immediately, or you have resources within yourself that survive such a moment.'
**Viktor Frankl**

'If you have built castles in the air--- put the foundations under them.'
**Thoreau**

'Words do not just reflect reality, the create reality.'
**'The Silva Mind Technique' José Silva**

'Realize, don't theorise.'
**Paul, private patient of Marianne**

'The war broke out... the world of nature was unaffected...flowers still bloomed, even butterflies still continued their migrations.'
**'Sweet Thames Run Softy' Robert Gibbings**

'Think work and act; don't sit here and brood amongst insoluble enigmas.'
**Henrik Ibsen**

'Without work all life goes rotten; but when work is soulless, life stifles and dies.'
**Albert Camus**

'Cheshire puss, would you tell me which way I ought to go from here?'
'That depends a good deal on where you want to get to'
**'Alice in Wonderland' Lewis Carroll**

'It's not wise to make life into hell by anticipating things that may never happen, nor, for that matter, by anticipating those that most surely will happen.'
**Robert Falcon Scott**

'The great human law—that merit is in the long run, recognised and rewarded.'
**'Up from Slavery' Booker T Washington**

Happiness

'It is activity which renders man happy.'
**Goethe**

'She was considering in her own mind—whether the pleasure of making a daisy chain would be worth the trouble of getting up and picking the daisies.'
**'Alice in Wonderland' Lewis Carroll**

'Life is a chain made up of many diverse links. Sorrow is one golden link between submission to the present and the promised hope of the future.'
**'The Prophet' Khalil Gibran**

'I would not have missed this time of poverty. One learns to value simple things.'
**'Memories Dreams and Reflections' Carl G Jung**

## Hope

'
Where there is much light, there is a darker shadow.'
**Goethe**

'Bear and endure; this sorrow will one day prove to be for good.'
**Ovid**

'There are certain times in our lives when we find ourselves in circumstances that...seem to weigh us down. They give us not only opportunity but impose the duty of elevating ourselves.'
**Goethe**

'Above the cloud with its shadow is the star with its light.'
**Victor Hugo**

'The sun is always shining above the clouds.'
**Marianne**

'He said not "thou shalt not be tempested", but that "thou shalt not be overcome.'
**Julian of Norwich**

## Maturity

'To be magnanimous – mighty of heart, is to be great in life; to become this increasingly is to advance in life.'
**Ruskin**

'If you wish a wise answer, you must put a rational question.'
**Goethe**

'He who asks timidly, courts refusal.'
**Seneco**

'We may measure our road to wisdom by the sorrows we have undergone.'
**Bulwer Lytton**

'If you do not err, you do not gain understanding.'
**Goethe**

'He who does not see the angels and devils in the beauty and malice of life, will be far removed from knowledge, and his spirit will be empty of affection.'
**Khalil Gibran**

'Everything can be taken from a man but one thing: to choose one's own way.'
**Victor Frankl**

'So many out of the way things had happened recently, that Alice began to think that few things indeed were impossible.'
**Lewis Carroll's Alice**

'To underestimate oneself is as much a departure from truth as to exaggerate one's powers.'
**'Sherlock Holmes' by A C Doyle**

'A man may conquer a thousand warriors, but the greatest of all is he who conquers himself.'
**Chinese saying**

Mental Health

'The mind is ever genius in making its own distress.'
**Oliver Goldsmith**

'The mind is its own place, and in itself, can make a heaven of hell, a hell of heaven.'

**John Milton**
'If you can't heal the wound, don't tear it open.'

**Danish Proverb**
'The world considers eccentricity in great things (to be) genius; in small things (to be) folly.'

**Bulwer Lytton**
'A mind that is free sees that dependency on (anyone) breeds fear.'

**Krishnamurti**
'Who am I then? Tell me that first, and then, if I like being that person

I'll come up; if not, I'll stay down here till I'm somebody else.'
**Lewis Carroll's 'Alice'**

## Relationships

'Where people are tied for life, 'tis their mutual interest not to grow weary of one another.'
**Lady Montagu (1930's)**

'If you would care to dislike a man, try to get nearer his heart.'
**J M Barrie**

"He who terrifies others, is himself in continual fear"
**Ovid**

"I could give you a basket of roses, but they would only fall;
I give you the flower of friendship, the most lasting gift of all"
**Marianne**

"A man, sir, should keep his friendships in constant repair"
**Dr Johnson**

"But if the while I think on thee dear friend, all losses are restored and sorrows end.'
**Shakespeare**

'I am a part of all that I have met. And a part of me belongs to all I meet.'

**Tennyson**
'If there's a secret to being loved, it lies in not having to be loved.'

**M Drury**

**Strength and Tenacity**

'The glory is not in never falling, but in rising every time you fall.'
**Bovee**

'Believe that each new day that shines on you is your last'
**Horace**

'Where difficulties are overcome, they become blessings"
**Traditional Saying**

**Anticipating Success**

'The seeds of today are the flowers of tomorrow.'"
**Unknown**

'Success is to be measured, not so much by the position that one has reached in life, as by the obstacles which he has overcome while trying to succeed'
**'Up From Slavery' by Booker T Washington**

"Where there is no hook, to be sure there will hang no bacon"
**Spanish Proverb**

'Who wills the end, wills the means'
**French Proverb**

If you have enjoyed these sayings you might like to read my new book on writing and producing your own *Book of Inspiration*.

# Chapter 14

## Further Information

---

Freud along with many others believed books give a unique insight into the working of the mind. There are no academic books which portray the human mind in torment and bliss but a rich seam is to be found in poetry, fiction and film.

It's no use recommending books I haven't read so forgive me if I miss any gems and tell me. It's good to receive positive feedback and learn new things.

There are many support groups but publishing national help line numbers creates a frustrating trail down to the local groups, the details of which are available in local libraries. I hope the following prove enjoyable reading to whet your appetite for further study into this fascinating field.

**ART WITH MEANING**
Psalms from the Bible
*Pure poetic expression of the joys and sorrows of living*

Selected Poetry of Kathleen Raine
*A fine metaphysical poet – I love her work*

Any paintings by William Blake
*An artist who successfully portrays madness, suffering and the human spirit*

The Plains of Heaven by John Martin
*One of his religious themed paintings; sit by it and enjoy the depth of experience it expresses*

Beyond Bedlam Published by Anvil Press
*Very moving poetry by patients of Bethlem Hospital.*

## BOOKS ABOUT LIFE
The Road Less Travelled by Scott Peck
*Self- improvement, by a very giving, generous man*

The Prophet - Khalil Gibran
*A beautifully written and moving prose poem about the meaning of life*

The Tao of Pooh by Benjamin Hoff
*An allegory about life, based on the children's characters.*

Jonathan Livingston Seagull by Richard Bach
*An allegory about daring to express individuality*

The House at Pooh Corner by A A Milne
*A children's book, with many lessons for adults about friendship and acceptance.*

Tono Bungay by H G Wells
*A life enhancing book with an allegory of how greed, success and failure finally bring peace to a man's life.*

The Door in the Wall by H G Wells
*A short story about belief and perceptions.*

Be Still and Know - The Miracle of Mindfulness by Thich Nhat Hanh
*A Taoist monk gives some very practical tips of how to enhance mundane experiences.*

## BIOGRAPHIES/DIARIES
The Diary of a Nobody by G & W Grossmith
*Two Victorian authors with a very funny book about ordinary experiences.*

The Horse Whisperer Nicholas Evans
*Read it as 'People Whisperer' and you'll learn lots.*

Anne Frank – the Diary by Anne Frank
*The moving and often amusing experiences of tragic Anne Frank, written shortly before she died in a concentration camp.*

## MENTAL ILLNESS
Dibs, in Search of Self by Virginia Axline
*How a lost child was brought back to the world by a Psychotherapist.*

Touched with Fire by Dr Kay Redfield Jamison
*Manic depressive illness – and creativity. A gem.*

DSM IV* Diagnostic & Statistical Manual of Mental Disorders
By American Psychiatric Association
*This is THE psychiatric diagnostic manual, as used by the Medical Profession.*

Final Exit by Dr Derek Humphry
*The controversial suicide manual written by a Doctor who helped his terminally wife end her life.*

The Man Who Thought His Wife Was a Hat by Dr Oliver Sachs
*Psychiatrist Sachs portrayals aphasia – an illness which prevents patients properly translating what they see.*

The History of Bethlem by J Andrews, J Briggs et al
*A primer for those interested in historical treatments.*

## FILM
### Shine
*The true story of garrulous pianist David Helfgott, who overcomes nervous breakdown to marry and play concerts in public.*

### Patch Adams
*A doctor dons a clown outfit and proves that laughter is as powerful a cure as any medicine.*

### Awakenings – based on the book by Dr Oliver Sachs
*The intensively moving portrayal of a Psychiatrist who successfully woke patients who had lain comatose for years after suffering encephalitis during the Influenza pandemic after the First World War.*

## WEBSITES
### Royal College of Psychiatrists
http://www.rcpsych.ac.uk/public/help/manicdep/man_frame.htm
*The following are the links to the key facts pages for a range of mental illnesses.*

Anxiety and phobia
http://www.rcpsych.ac.uk/mentalhealthinfo/problems/anxietyphobias/anxiety,panic,phobias.aspx

Being sectioned [under the Mental Health Act]
http://www.rcpsych.ac.uk/mentalhealthinfo/problems/beingsectionedengland.aspx

Bipolar disorder [formerly manic depressive psychosis]
http://www.rcpsych.ac.uk/mentalhealthinfo/problems/bipolardisorder/keyfactsbipolardisorder.aspx

bipolar [teenagers]
http://www.rcpsych.ac.uk/mentalhealthinfo/youngpeople/bipolardisorder/christinasstory.aspx

Community Mental Health Teams
http://www.rcpsych.ac.uk/mentalhealthinfo/treatments/communitytea
ms/keyfactscmhts.aspx

Depression
http://www.rcpsych.ac.uk/mentalhealthinfoforall/problems/depression/
depressionkeyfacts.aspx

Eating Disorders
http://www.rcpsych.ac.uk/mentalhealthinfo/problems/eatingdisorders/
eatingdisorderskeyfacts.aspx

electro convulsive therapy [ECT]
http://www.rcpsych.ac.uk/mentalhealthinfoforall/treatments/ect.aspx

Obsessive Compulsive Disorder [OCD]
http://www.rcpsych.ac.uk/mentalhealthinfo/problems/obsessivecompul
sivedisorder/ocdkeyfacts.aspx

Personality Disorders
http://www.rcpsych.ac.uk/mentalhealthinfo/problems/personalitydisor
ders/personalitydisordersfacts.aspx

Schizophrenia
http://www.rcpsych.ac.uk/mentalhealthinfoforall/problems/schizophre
nia/schizophreniakeyfacts.aspx

psychotherapies
http://www.rcpsych.ac.uk/mentalhealthinfo/treatments/psychotherapie
s.aspx

spirituality
http://www.rcpsych.ac.uk/mentalhealthinfo/treatments/spirituality.asp
x

## MENTAL HEALTH CHARITIES
American Internet Mental health
http://www.mentalhealth.com/

Bipolar UK [formerly Manic Depressive Alliance]
http://www.mdf.org.uk/

Depression Alliance
http://www.depressionalliance.org/

MIND mental health charity
http://www.mind.org.uk/

Rethink [formerly the National Schizophrenia Fellowship]
http://www.nsf.org.uk/

Anxiety UK [includes info on OCD]
http://www.anxietyuk.org.uk/about-anxiety/anxiety-
disorders/obsessive-compulsive-disorder-
ocd/?gclid=CM6EyrbvwK0CFUVTfAod_06DAw

## OTHER
Freud Museum
http://www.freud.org.uk/Index.html

School of Pharmacy web site
http://www.rgu.ac.uk/subj/pharmacy/pharmacy.htm

The story of Phineas Gage
http://www.guardian.co.uk/science/blog/2010/nov/05/phineas-gage-
head-personality
http://brightbytes.com/phineasgage/

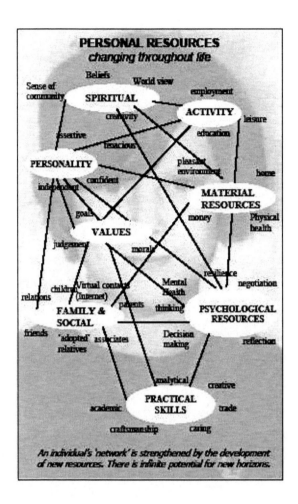

**PERSONAL RESOURCES**
*changing throughout life*

Beliefs
World view

Sense of
community

**SPIRITUAL**

employment

**ACTIVITY**

leisure

creativity

education

assertive

tenacious

**PERSONALITY**

pleasant
environment

home

confident

independent

**MATERIAL
RESOURCES**

goals

money

Physical
health

**VALUES**

judgement

morals

resilience

negotiation

children

Virtual contact
(Internet)

Mental
Health

relations

parents

thinking

**FAMILY &
SOCIAL**

**PSYCHOLOGICAL
RESOURCES**

friends

'adopted' associates
relatives

Decision
making

reflection

analytical

creative

**PRACTICAL
SKILLS**

trade

academic

craftsmanship

caring

*An individual's 'network' is strengthened by the development
of new resources. There is infinite potential for new horizons.*

## Glossary

### A

| | |
|---|---|
| acupuncture | Chinese treatment, for re-balancing energy |
| agoraphobia | fear of open spaces |
| anaesthetic | drugs rendering patient impervious to pain |
| analgesic | pain killing drug |
| ancestor worship | tribal culture of venerating their dead relatives |
| anorexia | eating disorder, restricts intake of food |
| anti psychotic | drug reduces symptoms of psychosis |
| anti social | difficulties in socialising |
| arachnaphobia | fear of spiders |
| archetype | character trait in personality (Jungian theory) |
| aromatherapy | a body massage with aromatic oils |
| asylum [Asylum] | place of refuge. institution for housing insane |
| autonomous | automatic systems e.g. breathing, heart, lungs |
| avoidant | characterised by 'avoiding' situations |

### B

| | |
|---|---|
| beck | rating for depressive illness |
| behaviour therapy | therapy aimed at modifying behaviour |
| Bethlem Asylum | 2nd oldest Hospital in UK; former Asylum |
| bi-polar | mental illness; alternating depression & mania |
| blood phobia | fear of blood or being infected by needles |
| borderline | mild personality disorder |
| brain chemistry | chemicals of brain distributed via transmitters |
| brief psychosis | short term episode of hallucinations, delusions |
| BPS | British Psychological Society |
| Broadmoor | Psychiatric Hospital for the criminally insane |
| bulimia nervosa | eating disorder of purging and vomiting |

### C

| | |
|---|---|
| Carl Jung | founder of Analytical Psychology |
| case history | history of patient's psychological and physical |
| catatonia | mental state characterised by total inertia |

| | |
|---|---|
| catharsis | 'purging'; 'letting go' of negative trait |
| CDPOM | drug dispensed on handwritten prescription |
| checking & testing | part of compulsive disorder 'checking' |
| chemical transmitter | way brain chemicals are distributed to cells |
| Chiropractic | manipulation; re-aligns skeletal system |
| Cinderella | Archetypal, representing innocence rewarded |
| claustrophobia | fear of confined spaces |
| Clinical Psychologist | Psychologist practices in a Hospital setting |
| cognitive-behavioural | recognition & changing behaviour patterns |
| compulsion | urge to carry out a certain act or ritual |
| contra indicative | reacts badly with chemicals (applied to drugs) |
| counselling | one of the talking cures |
| crimes of passion | crime committed during intense emotion |
| Cruse | charity providing free bereavement counselling |

D
| | |
|---|---|
| delusion | ideas perceived as real but are imagined |
| dependent | personality disorder - clinging to another |
| depressive | [illness] mental illness - hopelessness and sadness |
| DSM | Manual for diagnosing mental illness |

E
| | |
|---|---|
| ECT | Electro Convulsive Therapy treat chronic depressions |
| EEG | electro-encephalograph printed tape of brain activity |
| empathy | having an understanding of a personal situation |
| episode | period of mental illness |
| extraordinary | [perceptions] - what were taken as signs of madness |
| extrovert | outgoing, confident personality |

F

False memory [sydrome] disorder characterised by imagining events
that could not realistically have taken place

Forensic    criminal mental illness eg PPD

fragmenting' [of the mind] - see psychosis


G

genetic     cause is attributed to the inherited genes

grandiose   delusional belief e.g. believes he is God or a prophet

group       [therapy] conducted with Therapist and several
            patients

GSL         general sale list; drugs available for sale at a Pharmacy


H

Herbalist   therapist prescribes herbs

high        slang term to describe exaggerated emotions

histrionic  disorder characterised by exaggerated emotions

holistic    therapy which considers mind, spirit, and the body


I

imbalance   lack or excess of brain chemicals within the synapses

insanity    impaired state of mind sufferer out of touch with
            reality

insight     ability to understand the psychological situation

integrative using methods from more than one school of thought

interpret   [psychotherapy] - help patient gain insight introvert
            thinking, inward looking personality


J

Jungian     Analyst of the Jungian tradition.


L

leucotomy   psychosurgery, involving cutting frontal lobe of brain

lobotomy    see 'leucotomy'

Chancellor  Senior Judge in English Law

## M

Madhouse    Victorian; private hospitals for the insane

mania    mental illness, intense moods/ frantic behaviour

MAOI's    monoamine oxidase; anti depressive medication

medication    drugs given to c alleviate the symptoms of an illness

MIMS    manual of drugs and their characteristics, used by GPs

molecule    smallest particle of a particular chemical

mood swings (rapid) where a person's mood changes dramatically

muscle    relaxant drug to relax muscles, usually before surgery

mutagenicity ability of a drug to affect chemistry of organs

## N

narcissistic    personality disorder extreme self interest

## O

obsession    unhealthy preoccupation

obsessional    mental illness, obsessions and compulsions

'old lag'    commits petty crimes, in order to remain in prison

Osteopathy    therapy involving manipulation of spine

## P

panic attack sudden fear, usually onsets without warning

paranoia    extreme psychological fear

paranoid    form of schizophrenia

Patch Adams American Psychiatrist who uses humour therapy

persistent    unwanted ideas which will not go away

images    as above, but visual images

phobia    extreme fear

placebo test inert medication, part of drug trial tests

POM    prescription only drugs

Primary Care GP Surgery and all the practitioners who work there

psychosis    mental illness hallucinations and delusions

PTSD    stress disorder  occurs after traumatic event, accident

pow-wow    palaver; tribal meeting, to resolve social problems

Primary Care G.P.s and various therapists within G.P. Practices

psyche        [Greek] of the mind. After Goddess Psyche
Psychiatrist  Doctor with a qualification in Psychiatric Medicine
psychodrama therapy involving 'acting out' scenes from patient's
life
psychology   science of the study of human behaviour
psychomotor  agitation state of frantic activity as in manic episodes
psychopathic  personality disorder absence of a 'conscience'
psychosis     intense period of fear; mind unable to function
Psychotherapy talking cure; patient encouraged to develop 'insights'
put away      Victorian euphamism - locked in an Asylum


R
rhetorical    questions not answered directly but to trigger debate
ritual        ceremony to mark life changes e.g. birth, middle age
Royal College [of Psychiatrists]UK body of Psychiatrists


S
Samaritans    organisation to help suicidal people
scapegoat     animal /person sacrificed / to expiate sin of that society
schizoid      personality disorder detachment from society
schizophrenia fragmentation of personality,delusions, hallucinations
School        particular method of training - 'school of thought'
screws        [slang] Prison Warders
sectioned     [slang] detained under the Mental Health Act
serotonin     chemical transmitters in the brain
social misfit Victorian term; anyone committing social nuisance
social phobia fear of social situations
split         different personality characteristics in one person


T
talking cure  therapies use talking instead of drugs to effect a cure
tic           involuntary muscle movement, as in Tourettes
toxicity      level of toxin or poison
trauma        shock
trepanning    cutting of piece out of skull; primitive surgery

tricyclic    type of antidepressant; chemical structure 3 ('tri') rings
trip        [slang] hallucination induced by illegal drugs

V
voodoo      witchcraft ceremonies of a particular cult in Haiti

W
witch mark  16<sup>th</sup> century; areas with no feeling thought to be a
            mark of the devil. Now known as skin tags, a sign of
            ageing
word salad  babbling, as in forms of schizophrenia

## E-books in production by Marianne Richards

Create Your Own Book of Inspiration
We all need inspiration from time to time – here's how to create a beautiful and inspiring heirloom which will continue to comfort your descendants well into the future, as well as being on hand for your own difficult times. A practical book which contains a series of exercises - relaxations in themselves.

Beating the Bully – exposing the world of the bully
More than just 'how to', this comprehensive book draws useful, powerful parallels between bullying and 16th century witch hunting. Using examples of being bullied in the NHS and other organisations, the author offers hope and redemption - and the knowledge there is a future beyond the pain and despair.

Mental Illness and the Community, parts 1 & 2
Two comprehensive handbooks in one for new professionals and volunteers with an interest in mental illness. All you have ever wanted to know- and more in a handy little e-book packed with information and anecdotes. 2$^{nd}$ edition. These two books were first published by Emerald and still available in paperback.

My Family and Other Strange Creatures
The author's story of depression and autism - a family teetering on the edge and the profound effect it had on her life, loves, school, work and attitudes. Far more than misery memoir, it is an exploration of how 'being different' can be a blessing as well as a curse and lead to greater things. Told in a unique blend of prose, poetry, diagrams and photographic images which will move you from tears to laughter, from incredulity to delight. Contains strong language.

# Index

## A
Acupuncture, 182
Admission for Assessment, 69
Admission for Treatment, 70
Agitation. See 'psychomotor'
Agoraphobia, 169
Alchemy, 38
Anaesthetic, 93
Analgesic, 103
Anorexia Nervosa, 151
Anti Psychiatric Movement, 47, 61
Anti psychotic, 103
Anti social (Personality Disorder), 164
Antidepressants, 88, 103
Apothecary, 38
Approved Social Worker, 68, 69, 73
Arachnaphobia, 169
Aromatherapy, 182, 183
Art therapy, 139, 184
Asperger Syndrome, 65
Aubrey de Grey, 21
Automatic nervous system, 77
Autonomous, 77
Avoidant (Personality Disorder), 164

## B
Beck Depression Inventory, 148. See also 'BDI'
Bedlam, 41, 198
Behavioural therapy, 169
Behavioural Therapy, 158, 169, 174
Behaviourists, 47, 57

Belief - strongly held. See Delusion
Bethlem Asylum, 33, 43
Bi - Polar Illness, 157
Bi-polar (Mania & Depression), 155
Blood/infection phobia, 169
Bloodletting, 38
Borderline (Personality Disorder), 164
Brain chemistry, 143, 147
Brain Chemistry Imbalance, 88, 89
Brain fever, 37
Brief Psychotic Disorder, 142, 173
British Psychological Society, 123
Broadmoor, 137
Buddhism, 185
Bulimia nervosa, 151
Burrus Skinner, 57

C
Care in the Community, 13, 24, 41, 135, 136, 137
Carl Jung, 10, 54, 182
Carl Rogers, 60
Case history, 141
Catatonia, 173
Catatonic schizophrenia, 142
Catatonic Schizophrenia, 173
Catharsis, 52
Catholic Church, 10
Cerebral palsy, 42
Checking and testing. See also 'ritual'. See ritual
Chemical transmitters, 92
Chinese medicine, 25, 38, 182, 183
Claustrophobia, 169
Clinical Psychologists, 84

Cognitive Behavioural Therapies, 47, 60
Community Mental Health Team, 76, 82, 106, 129, 176
Complementary Practitioners, 177, 182
Compulsion, 160
Consent to Treatment, 71
Controller, 75
Counselling, 143
Counselling, 81, 84, 85, 129, 147
Criminality, 48
CRUSE, 114
Crystal Therapy, 185
Cultural factors, 172


D
Degeneration, 47, 48
Delusion, 143
Delusions, 173
Delusions, 173
Dependent (Personality Disorder), 164
Depression, 148, 156, 201, 202
Depressive illness, 146
Diagnoses, 75
Diagnostic and Statistics Manual (DSM), 79
Diagnostic Manual [DSM, 75, 79
Dialectical Behaviour Therapy (DBT), 47, 62
Doctor of Medicine (MD), 106
Drug addicts, 15
Drug Groups, 88, 101
DSM IV, 79
Dysfunctional, 164


E
Eating Disorder, 141, 151

Edward Thorndike, 57
EEG, 92
Egas Moniz, 51
Electric shock treatment (ECT, 40
Electro Convulsive Therapy (ECT), 88, 92, 147, 164
Electrodes, 93
Empathy, 85, 86
Energy, 158
Epilepsy, 42
Exclusion, 9, 13
Extrovert, 56

F
Family, 174
Fear - excessive or unreasonable. See 'Phobia'
Forensic work, 84
Fritz Perls, 60
Frontal Lobes, 51

G
Gardening therapy, 139
General Practitioner, 78
General Practitioners, (G.P.), 111
Genetic factor, 157
Giving an illness a name, 149
Grandiosity, 157
Group Therapy, 153
GSL – general sale list, 101

H
Hallucination, 103
Harold Shipman, 11, 24
Herbalist, 182
High, 155

Hippocrates, 33, 37, 38
Hypnosis, 47, 52

I
Imbalance in the brain chemistry, 148. See also 'brain chemistry'
Imbecility, 48, 49
Inquisitions, 10
Insanity, 9, 21, 48
Insight, 53
Intolerance, 9
Introvert, 56
Ivan Pavlov, 57

J
Jean Martin Charcot, 52
John Nash, 16, 142, 171
John Watson, 57
Joseph Breuer, 52

K
Keynote, 75

L
Labelling, 9, 14
Largactil, 58, 59
Lazar Houses, 42, 43
Leprosy, 42
Leucotomy, 51
Life event, 147
Lithium, 58, 59, 159
Living sculpture, 18
Lord Chancellor, 69

## M

Malfunction, 77
Mania, 37, 141, 155, 157
Manic. See mania
MAOI's (monoamine oxidase inhibitors, 104
Marina Tsvetaeva, 28
Marsha Lineham, 62
Massage, 182
Medical Practitioners, 88, 105
Melancholia, 37, 47, 50
Mental Health Act, 75
Mental Health Act - The, 145
Mental Health Act 1983, 5, 58, 67
Mental Health Managers (MHM), 69
Mental Health Rehabilitation Worker, 81, 86
Michel Foucault, 42
Milton Erickson, 47, 61, 85
MIMs, 100
Molecule, 95
Mood swings, 155
Moral Panics, 9, 11
Muscle relaxant, 93
Mutagenicity, 95

## N

Narcissistic (Personality Disorder), 164

## O

Obsession, 160
Obsessional Compulsive Disorder (OCD), 169
Obsessive Compulsive Disorder (OCD), 141, 160
Orderliness, 160
Organic brain disease, 42

Osteopathy, 184

P
Paranoid (Personality Disorder), 164
Paranoid Schizophrenia, 173
Persistent ideas, 160
Persistent images, 160
Persistent thoughts, 160
Personality Disorders, 162, 201
Pharmaceutical, 93
Pharmacist, 106, 107, 116, 117
Physiotherapy, 76
Plato, 40
Post traumatic Stress Disorder, 169
Post traumatic Stress Disorder (PTSD), 169
Prejudice, 9
Prostitution, 48
Psychiatric Hospital, 145
Psychiatrist, 17, 52, 61, 68, 69, 76, 78, 79, 93, 105, 106, 113, 118,
    145, 150, 178, 199, 200
Psycho Analysis, 158
Psycho Analyst, 82
Psychoanalysis, 53
Psychodrama, 139, 184
Psychomotor agitation, 157
Psychopath, 15, 174
Psychopathic (Personality Disorder), 164
Psychosis, 142
Psychosurgery, 47, 51, 88, 105
Psychotherapy, 81, 83, 153, 164, 169
Purging, 152
Purging, 38

## R

R D Laing, 21, 62, 178
Reflexology, 183
Registered Mental Nurse, 106, 113
Regression, 47, 52
Reichian Therapy, 184
Religious images, 171
Repressed sexual interest, 53
Richard Dadd, 50
Ritual, 160
Robert Gardiner Hill, 50
Royal College of Psychiatrists (RCP), 153

## S

Sadness, 148
Sadness and depression, 148. See also Depressive Illness
Samaritans, 138
Scapegoats, 35
Schizoid (Personality Disorder), 164
Schizophrenia, 15, 141, 171, 172, 201, 202
Sectioned, 145
Ssectioned, 68
Serotonin and noradrenaline, 103
Sigmund Freud, 10, 35, 52, 82
Situational phobia, 169
Sleep disturbance, 147
Social misfits, 13
Social phobia, 169
Social Work, 86
Speaking in tongues, 17
Spiritualists, 172
Split personality, 171
Sterility, 48

Stigmatisation, 22
Stimulant, 103
Stress, 143

T
Tangible, 149
Taoism, 185
Therapeutic Communities, 5, 135, 138, 139
Therapist, 81, 82, 114, 124, 174, 182, 184
Thomas Szaz, 62
Totalitarian states, 10
Toxicity, 95
Trauma, 143
Trepanning, 34
Tricyclic antidepressant, 103
Tricyclics, 103

V
Valium, 59
Victoria Climbie, 30
Vomiting, 152

W
Walter Freeman, 52
Warrant, 144
Warren Anatomical Museum, 51
William Cowper, 50
Word salad, 173

Y
Yoga, 177, 186